MW01602163

# Mental Models

*The Secret Weapon to Master Problem Solving, Boost Your Productivity, and Make Better Decisions*

By Charlie Holl

# Table of Contents

# Introduction

Hi, my name is Charlie Holl and welcome to *Mental Models: The Secret Weapon to Master Problem Solving, Boost Your Productivity, and Make Better Decisions.*

You've already taken one step forward toward a better future by merely opening up the book. Everyday we walk through life, pushing forward, making choices, settling on decisions, and powering through the tough moments. We do all of this while in the back of our minds we are coloring our hair, thinking about school lunches, trying to remember the doctor appointments we scheduled, and deciding whether to cook chicken or spaghetti for dinner.

Our brains are amazing, wonderful, and powerful parts of our bodies, but they can also be stubborn and controlling. When we choose to go through life making choices based on the ideals learned while we were children, hidden for most of our lives, we struggle with making unbiased decisions without even really knowing that we're doing it.

What we don't realize is that those very thoughts are actually structured in our brains as a mental model. In other words, each thought is a naturally constructed mental model with no specific guidance on how we want things to steer. Within this book, you're going to have the chance to learn a lot about specific and purposeful types of models, as well as the best way to begin expanding your mind, boosting your productivity, and making better decisions.

We'll start with Chapter One, giving a full clinical definition of mental models. This specific type of problem solving technique has been used for decades by some of the most well-known entrepreneurs in history. Of course, this isn't the first time anyone famous has talked about mental models. Warren Buffett has spoken of them for years, giving the models credit for a huge portion of his success throughout his life.

Continuing on in Chapter One, we will talk about the psychology behind mental models. We will list the seven principles of reason realized by Johnson-Lair and Savary in 1996. The models represent a base and a scientific infrastructure from which to conduct research. The principles also better explain the inner workings of the mental models. We will then finish up Chapter One with a brief explanation of why we use the models. This type of methodical tool has been adopted across almost all professions, including scientists, mathematicians, doctors, behaviorists, psychologists, and others. Corporations teach the power of mental models to employees and use them during team projects.

Once you have a good handle on what mental models are, you'll be able to begin processing the different types of them that are out there. The thing about mental models that is different than other tactics used for productivity, problem solving, and decision making is the fact that these tools come from inside your head. You don't need to spend money on some system or extensive training; you conceive the model in your own mind and use it to reach your goals. Literally anyone can use mental models, but it's not the fact that you can use them that is important; it's how you use them that matters.

In Chapter Two, we begin by talking about improving your vision using the techniques employed in this book. We discuss the mental pictures that you can create in your head, and we discuss how many mental models are out there compared to the simple one that you use on a daily basis to solve your everyday small problems.

Chapter Two delves into the idea of immersing yourself in the multiple variations of mental moods. It's a fact that if you choose to use the one known and created mental model, you won't come anywhere near the options and benefits you would if you chose the mental model based on the project. One of the main reasons that we use mental models in problem solving and decision making is to allow ourselves to explore beyond what our normal minds would allow and to see the multitude of opportunities to solve a problem or make a decision. Issues in life are not black and white or cut and dry, so why would we use tactics to handle them that are?

It has long been said that a person's own view of the world or biases can be the killer of business decisions. Mental models help you to circumnavigate some of those issues. Further into Chapter Two, we will talk about some of the more widely used mental models and the principles of each. We cover common knowledge, diversification, game theory, anchoring heuristic, the illusion of control, tribalism, working backward, and homeostasis. While these are only a few of the hundreds, if not thousands of mental models out there, they are the most pertinent and widely used tactics.

Backtracking a bit to talk about human nature and our brains,

Chapter Three will cover something that has affected even the most brilliant people. Cognitive bias can creep up on you in the strangest moments, and it can take affect without you ever realizing. Once you fully understand what cognitive bias is, you will be able to look back over the years and think about all of the situations in which you made a choice, now fully aware that it was based on your own personal biases. It's sometimes painful to look back, knowing that there were hundreds of other ways that decisions could have been made. With that being said, unfortunately, there is no time machine for a do-over.

We will also talk about how cognitive bias actually works in the chapter. Our minds are not infinite, and our brains can only hold so much data at one time. Therefore, when we begin to take in an overload of information, our brains push the other information out or stores it in our subconscious. However, your mind does not understand the difference between a fact about the current project and your distracted thoughts on the newest shoes from your favorite designer. What the brain does know is that there are chemical endorphins and upped serotonin levels that react in our bodies when we are thinking about something that we enjoy, and let's face it, the newest episode of Game of Thrones can be a heck of a lot more engaging for our brains then solving a problem.

Chapter Three then comes to a closure after touching briefly on the four causes of cognitive bias and the comparison with logical fallacy. Pay close attention to this part, because they are two different things, and logical fallacy is not going to produce the results you are looking for through mental modeling.

Just like the different models that mental modeling has to offer, there are various types of cognitive bias. A lot of these biases can play a role in distracting you from your mental models, but there are some that you can twist to adhere to your own specific needs for a project. Also, just like mental modeling, cognitive bias can happen anywhere and at any time. Unlike mental modeling, this means that you need to think about these biases long before you attempt to implement mental modeling into your life.

There is both confirmation bias and heavy weighted anchor biases, including everything in between. While we could write an entire book on the different types of cognitive bias alone, we put the most pertinent information into Chapter Four. We go over the ambiguity effect, confirmation bias, availability heuristic, halo effect, the self-serving bias, attentional bias, actor-observer bias, functional fixedness, anchoring bias, misinformation effect, false consensus effect, optimism bias, automation bias, and finally, courtesy bias.

The important thing to know about all of these biases is that if you suffer from their effects, they are not incurable. It will take strength, wisdom, and time to change the way your mind works, but you will be able to push past any deep seated bias that you might have. Remember that you are doing all of this to improve the quality of your life, relieve stress, improve a work environment, and to stay healthy long into old age.

Let's be honest here; we could spend days talking circles around cognitive bias such as what causes it, why you believe some things versus others, the morality of bias, and so on and so forth, but that would be useless. The majority of our lives (outside of sleep) is spent in motion. We are a productive species that doesn't like to sit still for very long. We don't like to have tasks hanging over our heads. So, we move on that. We try waves of improving our daily productivity, our problem solving skills, and our ever important decision making skills. These are the majority of actions that all human beings follow.

We move on to the depth of mental model use. We talk about

the fact that not all issues require a full-scale mental model. Some of them are solved by our own processes before we can even fully comprehend the issue. There is a process for these types of decisions and issues and it all starts with defining the problem that you are facing.

From there, you begin generating solutions to the problems If you use the first thing that pops into your mind you might have lost out on lucrative opportunities. After the solutions are generated, then you evaluate all of the options and select the ones you want. Ultimately, you implement that choice. As stated above, this whole process might not take you more than fifteen seconds, but it is still firmly in place.

From here, we begin to talk about productivity and two of the mental models that are used the most often - the Pareto principle and the 2-minute rule. Problem solving is next in Chapter Five, covering both the inversion mental model and Occam's razor, comparing how the two have any bearing on the world outside of their countries or personal attitudes. Last, but definitely not least, Chapter Five dives into decision making and provides an in-depth look into the mental models that shaped one of the richest men in the world, Warren Buffett.

As with any process on the market or in the business manuals, there will be both best practices to follow as well as things you want to avoid when implementing mental modeling. Success pushes all of us in some way or another. Whether you are a thriving parent or a CEO of a company, the best practices and avoidances stay the same across the board. Your financial status and specific career play no part in how the mental models play out or how the personal cognitive bias affects you.

The first set of best practices that we discuss center around success. Since it is one of the major drivers within us, we want to make sure that the actions we take on a daily basis point our sails in that direction. We cover productivity, messy workspaces, 90-minute power work, overworking yourself, efficiency, afternoon naps, and the importance of healthy diet habits and physical activity.

From there, we will move on to problem solving practices. From your daily routine to issues with projects at work, we are constantly problem solving. In this section, we talk about creating and evaluating systems, creating a positive mindset no matter the outcome or challenge, a change of perspective, and self-evaluations. All of these best practices can really help you improve on your mental model processing.

Decision making best practices come next with a complete description of how to handle too many hands on a project, the training of employees in best decision making tactics, and how checklists can help you organize your decision making processes. We then finish out the chapter by discussing the major things that you must avoid when attempting to get the full effects of best practices added to mental modeling.

Chapter Seven goes in-depth on the ever evolving and growing world of team mental model processes. We cover studies that have been done and the difficulty researchers experience pulling real data. The good news is that it seems to be working out for the best. When following a strong routine and having full participation, the company is opening up their problem-fixing abilities tenfold. Teams all on the same mental model process come up with over 50 percent more possible options for fixing problems and reaching decisions then one single person implementing the same process. Teams allow for all expertise across the board to come together and learn and grow from each other while implementing the best possible choices in a project.

Also in Chapter Seven, we will go over the mental model team's best practices. Under this section, we cover the importance of role assignments within the team dynamic. We talk about the widening of perspectives and the sharing of information within the team. Then, we end Chapter Seven with an explanation of the importance of asking the whats, whys, and hows within the group setting to have a firm grasp on why the ultimate situation was made.

The last chapter in the book attempts to wrap up all of the information you learned up to that point and bring the discussion back to a personal level. Whether you are modeling on your own or within a group, you still have to personally perfect your mental modeling processes. This is not a tool that others can do for you and your participation is just as vital as everyone else's. We discuss our growth from children, the systematic fear of our bosses, and the responsibilities of upper management to nip that in the butt. From there, we finish up with a look at that individual ability to change your personal mental model.

Within this section, Senge's ladder of inference is shown, giving a good explanation of how the normal human being sees the world around them, at least from a cognitive view. These perspectives will help you understand how to begin to challenge your own beliefs and cognitive bias.

By the end of *Mental Models*, you are going to have a very solid grasp on the process, best practices, avoidable actions, and ways by which to implement them into your own life. Don't forget that whether you are traditionally employed or not, mental models can bring new opportunities into the picture and allow you to fully embrace a new way of thinking.

# Chapter One: What Are Mental Models?

We use mental models every single day. We make decisions, organize our lives, and strive to become even more productive then the last day without knowing we organize, compartmentalize, and instruct ourselves on how to accomplish the tasks that we've set out to accomplish. What we don't think about is the fact that when we are subconsciously micromanaging ourselves, we are actually using a form of mental modeling. The Interaction Design Foundation explains mental modeling as follows:

> *Mental models are an artefact of belief. They are the beliefs that a user holds about any given system or interaction. In most instances, the belief will – to a certain extent – resemble the real life model. This is important because users will plan and predict future actions within a system based on their mental models.* (Int. Design Found., 2015)

When we're at work, we run through the tasks we have to complete, putting them in order according to importance, by making lists, and by noting the plethora of other simple tasks we use to accomplish the larger ones. Throughout history, CEOs, businesspeople, managers, and even entry level employees have used mental modeling to create a workflow that is timely and efficient. As time has passed, those steps in our heads have become major tools for lucrative business practices.

## Psychology of Mental Models

At their core, mental models are phrenic representations of theoretical and imaginary processes. They are concepts and views that you have locked in your mind, allowing you to better understand relationship qualities of almost everything you come across in the world. It's your brain working out how things work. In 1886, a philosopher named Charles Sanders Pierce explained reasoning and the process of it in a very specific manner. He said that humans examine the actual state argued in the proposition, they form charts, consciously visualize the parts of the charts that aren't given in the initial proposal, find a comfortable assertion of understanding from the mental models showing that the conditions would always exist, and come to the conclusion of truth.

To further this theory, the Scottish psychologist, Kenneth Craik, thought of a similar idea in 1943. He theorized that those concepts in people's heads were "small-scale models" of what the person expected the result to be. Since then, psychologists have discussed these mental models and how we put them to work, even from childhood; however, no theory would be a true scientific one without specified principles to guide it.

## Principles of Reason

In 1996, Johnson-Laird and Savary came up with a foundational principle of mental models that states that people who reason the events exhibit or show as little of the information as they possibly can in explicit models and end up representing on that which is true.

To further explain this concept, they created the principal assumptions of the theory:

1. **Every model is a key to possibilities.**

2. **The model relates to the specific subject at hand.** The model itself is specific to what the person is working on..

3. **Models explain assumption, introduction, and interpretation**. For assumption tasks, all models are possible. For an introduction task, the model is chosen

based on the understanding of that theory. In interpretations, you will find new mental models being created to fit the scope of the process.

4. **The theory gives two sides of the fence.** One process is going to be extremely rigid and allow very little change. The second process will move, shape, and fit to solve the problem.

5. **The more models that are required, the harder it will be to solve.**

6. **Mental models only represent the truth.**

In the 2002 paper, *The Cognitive Basis of Model-Based Reasoning in Science*, psychologist Nersessian questioned whether mental modeling was a short term immediate cognitive function or part of long term memory. That debate has continued in the psychological world, but it is known that whichever it falls under ( possibly both), it is a tool that is used on a regular basis and not always consciously.

## Why We Use Mental Models

Mental models are as natural to humans as eating, sleeping, walking, and talking. We are constantly processing the things around us, from colors to the most recent enlightened sermon you watch on YouTube. These models are the basis of your perception and how you react to things in life. They are your very fundamental tools for thinking. With these tools, you solve your everyday problems, you create an understanding of life and the world around you, and you systematically make decisions based on your own feelings and background.

When it comes to using these mental models for work, research, and medicine, we know that there isn't one perfect model for everything. In fact, there isn't a perfect one period. If you look at astrophysics, there has never been a process model that has allowed us to understand every single thing about the universe, what happened before the big bang, or what will come after our time here. However, the models seem to be efficient enough; they have led us through time, allowing us to create some of the most important aspects of modern society.

We have built bridges to cross the waters and roads to make our travel easier and faster. We have developed technologies that just 50 years ago seemed ridiculous. We put a man on the moon, we circled the earth in a rocket ship, and we cured many deadly diseases of the world. Scientists use these models, entrepreneurs use the models, and parents use the models. These are universal, but each individual model is formed to fit its specific genre of thought.

The best ones have a wide utility. They are capable of being used from the home, the lab, and the office building. Naturally, we as people automatically use whatever mental model is the best for us. These models allow us to think, to rationalize the world around us, and to effectively walk through life solving problems, creating great big things, and building the experiences we have.

What we don't realize is the importance of broadening our knowledge about the different types of mental models out there. When we automatically fall into what is comfortable, it can inhibit us from fully reaching our potential. We use the same model over and over, but it is not always (and often is not) the model we need to be implementing.

Biologist Robert Sapolsky explained this theory by asking the following question: "Why did the chicken cross the road?" He then revealed the answers that several different experts in different fields provided.

1. If you ask an evolutionary biologist, they might say, "The chicken crossed the road because they saw a potential mate on the other side."

2. If you ask a kinesiologist, they might say, "The chicken crossed the road because the muscles in the leg contracted and pulled the leg bone forward during each step."

3. If you ask a neuroscientist, they might say, "The chicken

crossed the road because the neurons in the chicken's brain fired and triggered the movement." Clear, (Date Unknown)

What people don't realize is that while none of them are wrong, none of them are fully correct either. They are all answering the question based on their own world view. It is almost impossible to step back out from that and look at the larger picture, but to fully solve a problem or complete a project, it is imperative to look at it from a broad range. In Zat Rana's piece in Design Luck on Charlie Munger, they stated that to get the most out of models, there are three basic principles that are always true, which are detailed below.

1. Our lives center around complexities of mass proportions and are built upon the connections and interactions of infinite variables. It is true that we can turn the odds of success to our favor by certain actions that twist the variables, our brains themselves don't understand which ones are important and which are not. Mental models are the bridge over this gap.

2. From birth, our brains are formulated to know the world through the idea of cause and effect. Because we aren't opening up to a broader idea, we are closing our ability to think short and putting ourselves in possible harm. Mental models target those holes - those blind spots in our brain's thoughts - in order to keep us from

making errors in our judgement process.

3. Mental models need to be diverse, especially in one's own personal collection. A multidisciplinary approach is the optimum way to dissect the theories and ideas around us. Humans must learn to understand the processes and ideas within the core subjects in order to move life into the direction they desire, and it reduces the possibility that we are relying on just one idea that could easily be wrong.

This is when you reach the point of having to learn how to think, construct, and imagine using more than just one tool. This can be difficult, especially after years of using your most comfortable instruments. It is possible, though, and expanding that repertoire of knowledge can open you up to an entire new world.

# Chapter Two: Making Mental Models Work For You

It is possible to go through life without ever broadening your mental model horizon, but it will be nearly impossible to make the choices that are thought out and perfectly assimilated for the situations and tasks that you face throughout your life. With these mental models, you will be able to broaden your horizons, allowing everything to work to its best ability. Your life, your career, and your choices will all fall into the perfect order if you are capable of relinquishing those modeling ideals that you created when you were just a child.

James Clear, author, entrepreneur, and photographer, explained the importance of broadening and expanding your mental modeling to improve your vision. He said that each one of our eyes can see images on their own. However, if you cover one of them up, you lose part of the image. Therefore, it is impossible to see an entire image or picture with only one eye open.

If you think about it, our mental models are giving us that

psychological, internal picture of how the world works and how you work inside of it. If the world is constantly changing and evolving, wouldn't your need to change your mental modeling technique do the same? After all, you wouldn't critique the motor of an engine the same way you would critique a dish from a five-star restaurant; it would be an entirely different process altogether. In order to fully enlighten yourself on your options, you will have to put in some work. You will need to learn the fundamentals of fields and careers that don't really relate to you at all. If mental modeling comes from your own worldview, to broaden it, you will need to learn from people who have completely different views from you.

That mental picture that you create in your head needs a plethora of different perspectives to really pull from. The more perspectives you have opened yourself up to, the better the end picture will be. You will be able to think and process the world, ideas, and problems from a spectrum much broader than your own tiny bubble. This will allow you to fully understand the different avenues and choices that you have available to you.

In *Mental Models* by James Clear, he explains that creativity and creation usually happen at that moment ideas are being born. This is exactly why the appreciation and understanding for other modeling techniques and viewpoints is essential. When we are children, our lives are segmented. We learn life skills as a baby in large chunks of segmented time created by our parents. Each sector has some other objective.

When we reach school, that doesn't stop, going on until the moment we leave college for the last time. We pick our courses - specified segmentations of knowledge. However, when you enter the world, you find that the majority of highly successful people do not think in that segmented fashion; they have pulled together the different models, looked at different perspectives through life, and have put them all together in their minds. They are able to flow from one subject to the next, creating that connection that you usually wouldn't even realize was there.

Also, when you understand these mental models and how they can work with each other, you will be able to find ideas and solutions in those intersections. These are the ideas and theories that very few people will actually come up with. Only those able to freely flow from idea to idea will be capable of doing so. Although, you don't have to know every single one - just the main models originating from the primary sectors of life, such as biology, chemistry, physics, economics, philosophy, psychology, and mathematics. These are the basic building blocks to our lives and of our moving and evolving society.

# Types of Mental Models and Principles of Each

There are very specific mental models used by some of the most famous people in the world, but those will be discussed later in the book. It is important to get a firm grasp on the most widely used and the broadest mental models used throughout life. These mental models can be applied to the business sector they are labeled with, but they can also be utilized in everyday life. Don't forget that mental models are not just for work, but for everything else in your life as well. Here are some of the most common mental models and how they can be implemented.

## Common Knowledge

Common knowledge is used by everyone every day. It is the general information, the facts, and the understandings that almost everyone has. This mental model does not have to fit into any one specific category. It can be used across all subjects of life, from economics and entertainment, to math, science, and history. This information is always accepted as fact, usually because it is an idea of creation that almost everyone knows and can agree on. Some examples of these are the temperature water freezes, the rotation speed of the earth, how many inches there are in a foot, and so on and so forth.

The scientific method is a technique that is used in order to decide what is the real truth, and what is a societal construct or falsity aligned inside of common knowledge. This technique is primarily used in math, astronomy, physics, and the laws of nature. Within our judicial system, hearsay usually draws its facts based on common knowledge and, therefore, it is often excluded from evidence.

## Diversification

This term is widely used in the world of finance. You probably have heard it spoken many times through life, especially in regards to investment portfolios. Diversification is the act of allocation of capital in a specific way to ultimately reduce exposure of any specific assets. There are several different techniques when it comes to diversification, but the main goal is to reduce risk.

Diversification as a mental model plays out with the investor. Understanding the market and the movement of it is key to successfully implementing the diversified investments. The size of diverse interactions within the financial account is limitless but has to be played out in just the right sequence in order to fully bring in the maximum amount of financial positives possible.

## Game Theory

Game theory is applicable to a broad range of relations and is currently used as an umbrella term for the science of logical decision making in people, computers, and even animals. Game theory can be traced back to the 1930s, but the 50s were when it was extensively developed by scholars. In the 1970s, it was put into motion in biology but is now thought of as a very important tool in several different fields of study. There are multiple techniques, or types, of game theory, including the following:

- Cooperative/non-cooperative

- Zero sum/non-zero-sum

- Simultaneous/sequential

- Perfect and imperfect information

- Combinatorial games

- Infinitely long games

- Discrete and continuous games

- Differential games

- Evolutionary game theory

- Stochastic outcomes

- Metagames

- Pooling games

- Mean field game theory

The games must always include specific elements. You need to have a player in the game, the actions available to them, the information available to them, and the payoff for the action. All of these can be internalized and thought about in a strategic mental view.

## Anchoring Heuristic

Anchoring is used mostly in psychology, but it can also be a negative model if used without understanding the premise. Anchoring occurs when a decision has been brought to the table and the decider makes the choices based on one initial piece of information they have received. This is especially common in situations of emotion or stress.

Anchoring heuristic is the psychological heuristic where people assess probability. They start with the anchor or the reference point that is given to them and then make changes and adjustments to it until they are able to reach a conclusion. The changes are usually very small, which gives the anchor a strong influence in the assessment. This heuristic was theorized by Daniel Kahneman and Amos Tversky, both of whom completed many studies on the subject.

## The Illusion of Control

The Illusion of control is when a person makes a choice or solves a problem based on the idea that they have more control than they actually do over the event. Psychologist Ellen Langer named the theory, which is implemented by combining three main points of interest and evidence:

1.  Lab experiments

2.  Observed behavior in games of chance

3.  Real-world behavior

From Langer's experiments, he drew the conclusion that

people acted more in control when they were tested on skills rather than fact. These skills included choice, competition, familiarity, and outside stimuli. You can often find this type of behavior within institutions of gambling.

## Tribalism

When it comes to mental models, the concept of tribalism has a great deal to do with loyalty. While it could be loyalty to their tribe or social group, it can also be any sort of loyalty used when making a choice or completing a project. When you use your brain to figure things out, you might find that, regardless of the world views you possess, you are likely to include your own world view and the world view of people very similar to you when making a decision or brainstorming ideas. This is a difficult thing to overcome, and it is a psychological aspect of mental modeling.

## Working Backward

Working backward is also known as "backward chaining". This type of mental model is a thinking model used in computer systems. It is the act of working backward from the solution. Artificial intelligence systems use this type of model in order to compute outcomes for the data input into the system. This is the most often used method of reasoning and is utilized with inference from other rules and logical assumptions.

If a person were to use this model, they would have to be experienced in the issue they were looking to solve. It would be difficult to work your way back with a problem if you have no idea how to get there. This is both mathematical and psychological.

## Homeostasis

Homeostasis is also known as "equilibrium", a term coined by Walter Bradford Cannon in 1926. However, the person to initially create the concept was French physiologist Claude Bernard almost 60 years beforehand. Bernard described the problem as such:

> *Homeostasis is the property of a system within an organism in which a variable, such as the concentration of a substance in solution, is actively regulated to remain very nearly constant. Examples of homeostasis include the regulation of body temperature, the pH of extracellular fluid, or the concentrations of sodium, potassium, and calcium ions, as well as that of glucose in the blood plasma,*

*despite changes in the environment, diet, or level of activity. Each of these variables is controlled by a separate regulator or homeostatic mechanism, which, together, maintain life.* Bernard, (1865)

This type of mental model is used in biology on a regular basis.

There are literally hundreds of other mental models out there, but we have highlighted some of the most used models. A few other models include the atomic theory, leverage, power laws, critical mass, relativity, and velocity. While using mental models, you must be thorough and knowledgeable. Sometimes, when in a hurry or in a frustrated mood, a cognitive bias can work its way up to the front of your mind.

# Chapter Three: Cognitive Bias

When you are in the middle of a mental model, moving and shifting the vision of the completed project or outcome, you are causing all of the pieces to fit together perfectly. In the optimal situation, the only information flowing through your head would be the facts given and the processes necessary to come to a conclusion. However, we have human brains, and they don't just store facts and processes like a computer would; this is where cognitive bias plays an instrumental and often damaging role in our choices and the flow inside of our mental models.

A cognitive bias is essentially an error in the way that we think that affects our decision making skills as well as our judgment. One of the first ways that it is affected is through our own personal bias. Memories that are stored in our brain of a similar event that may have created a bias will lead to that altered bias thinking and decision making. These biases could throw an entire process off, leading to a choice that is not in the optimal range for the mental model.

Another cognitive bias that we struggle with is our attention span. In a world filled with distractions, technology, and a constantly evolving movement, it is easy to lose that attention when processing through your mental model. These distractions can also create biases that are subconscious. For example, if you are creating a grocery list, going through the financial steps, the listing, and the decision process, and you hear a commercial for a specific brand of cereal, that may affect your choice. You may remember eating cereal as a child, the memory floating back through your head. That memory could invoke an emotion that will ultimately sway your decision making based on emotion rather than fact.

Think about how many different thoughts flow through your mind at any given moment. While just sitting around reading this book, your mind will pick up on cues from the words, spiraling outward. You may have just thought about your favorite cereal, having to do your grocery shopping, or even circumstances that you have related to your own life. All of these things come into your mind like noise, distracting you from the facts and the choices that you are presenting yourself with in your mental models. Why is it that we do this? How exactly do we get so easily distracted?

# How Does Cognitive Bias Work?

We know that cognitive bias is an error in our thought processes while we are processing decisions, interpreting new information, and setting up the base of our mental model. The whole world can act like an error in our thinking. Our brains, regardless of their power and capabilities still have limitations to them. When you have a million things going on in your mind, your brain begins to shut down or block certain parts from your conscious thought. It is attempting to simplify the process of quantifying the information that you are trying to focus on. The problem is, your brain doesn't know which information is pertinent and which is not when you are thinking of a million different things.

That processing is supposed to help you make sense of your task, and of the world as it relates to it. Your brain also knows you are trying to make these decisions in a short amount of time. There are always deadlines in life, and we can't just sit here and let them glide away in our brains forever. So, our brains take that concept and adjust the speed in which it deletes and pushes back information, just not always the correct information.

Our moral compass is always at work, and always pointing in the direction we would like to believe we encompass. We want to make decisions that are objective of bias, logical in scope, and thorough with the information that has been given. When we are distracted, overwhelmed, anxious, or inattentive, those biases that we try so hard to push out, creep in a little at a time. Almost always, you are not conscious of those biases when you reach a decision about something. So, they are left in your decision making models and end with unfruitful decisions and judgments not based in fact and objective truth. Ultimately, you are making bad decisions.

## Causes of Cognitive Bias

We have gone over the obvious causes of cognitive bias - attention and personal biases - but when you reach beyond those, there are four very common biases that can affect anyone in regards to making choices. These causes are universal across all types and sectors of mental modeling, and they affect cognitive bias even when attention and personal bias are not an issue. Let's take a look at these four common causes.

# An Overabundance of Information

If you look at the world as a whole and how long human beings have been on it collecting data and evolving information, it becomes quite clear that no one can know or even process all of it. An overabundance of information can come from the general view that there is just far too much information out there for us to process. While humans have a tendency to tell themselves that they can do anything they put their mind to, there are limitations.

Your senses are the collectors of information, taking in data by using sight, hearing, smell, taste, and touch. We are constantly inputting and outputting, just like the computers that we ourselves created. However, on top of that, we live in a very large place. We live in houses, neighborhoods, towns, counties, states, countries, hemispheres, on a planet in the solar system, and in the universe. From there, we don't know. For all we know, we are just a speck of sand in an extended and twisted multiverse. The amount of knowledge within those spaces is astronomical. It is nearly impossible to believe that it could be picked up by one person.

In fact, even here on our own planet, deep in the ocean, far into the trenches of the rainforests, we are still discovering new species of plants and animals. It is obvious that even if we were capable of taking in the information from all of these places, we would undoubtedly miss some. This is a fault of sorts - an evolutionary blockage that we have - and we will pass it on to other humans and to the artificial intelligence that we surround ourselves with.

As humans, we have to come to the conclusion that we are okay with the fact that we will never be able to understand everything that is out there. Our species is not large enough to fully grasp the power of that type of knowledge, and our reach is currently far too short to even try. The overabundance of information is hardly ever a blessing, and it is too often a distraction from what we should be focusing on.

## Connecting the Dots

Once you have collected all of that data - that raw information that you are either given, taught, or already knew - you have to do something with it. We, as humans, with the great power of our brains compared to other species, process that information into meaningful data. In order to do that, we have to take two sides and figure out how to connect the dots between them. On one side, we have the limited raw data and information we collected, and on the other side, we have the numerous mental models, our personal beliefs, professional beliefs, symbols, biases, and associations from when the situation had found us in the past.

When you connect the dots, you are often doing it without any information to back you up. You will connect them together in the best way possible by using your preconceived ideas, history, and personal convictions as the thread. When you are through, you have this mental model created from your own brain that is a combination of new information and old information. These new stories or decisions are based off of the fact that you began to tether the ideas together the best you could. In reality, though, these new ideas will be seething with past information. They will not be clear and concise.

## Time Is of the Essence

Time seems to be a constant theme in our lives. When we are young, we can't wait for time to go by, wanting to become adults, have jobs, and be someone of importance. Then when we reach the lackluster reality of it all, and we wish for time to speed up so we can get to retirement to enjoy our older years like we so richly deserve. However, somewhere in there, between the meetings and the marriage, the children and the corporate meetings, we realize that time is actually finite.

There is no real difference when it comes to decisions. No matter what model we use, no one, not even a computer, could sit and go through every single option for the issue at hand. While some things might seem like they are cut and dry, statistically speaking, that is not the case. It would take multiple lifetimes just to decide what you wanted for breakfast if you had to think of every option out there. Considering your life is a pretty important resource, that would run out long before you actually finished looking at the choices - and you'd be pretty hungry.

## Human RAM

So, for argument's sake, let's assume that you could take in all the information out there on your subject, you could turn and process it into meaningful, bias-lacking, information, and you had super speed when you did it. There is still one really huge problem - our brains do not have the space to hold all the information, all our symbolism, all our stories, and all of our past choices. Our brains know that there is limited space in there, and that, ultimately, it has to let some things go in order to keep the important information there.

Am I saying this is why we constantly lose our keys? No, but if you have a very mentally demanding job, that could play a part. If the information is small, and it clears up space for what you are working on in that moment, your brain will kick it to the curb - or at least store it in that subconscious so when you go looking for them, it drives you crazy because you know you know where you put them, but you just can't pull that memory.

Oftentimes, a way we pull in more information when our brains are bulging is by generalizing the facts, identifying patterns within the data so we don't have to remember every word, and by trying to compartmentalize everything in there. However, if you do that, aren't you basically defeating the purpose of pulling all that information in the first place? Now you've dumbed it down without knowing if you'll be able to retrieve it when you need to. While it seems we made computers in our image (minus the emotional stuff), they aren't superbots either. They only have a certain amount of storage space, and sometimes, it'll start deleting if you don't keep up with it.

Now, because both cognitive bias and logical fallacies can come into play in mental models, let's clear up what the two are and how they are different.

## Cognitive Bias vs. Logical Fallacy

Seeing as we now know all about cognitive bias, we should begin to understand its buddy, logical fallacy. They are not the same. Many psychologists and philosophers have debated the differences between the two, but in the end, both have a very distinct definition. At the same time, one can also be malicious in nature.

A logical fallacy is a common error in reason that undermines the logic and truth of your argument. These fallacies can fall in line with illegitimate arguments and ones that don't even closely resemble the issue being talked about. They can also spew their point of view but have absolutely no evidence or completely biased evidence to back them up. It seems that in this day and age of tumultuous politics, people find themselves battling back and forth, having negative information thrown at them without any type of explanation or proof. Most of the time, it's personal emotion mixed with media bias. Either way, it's not a good combination.

Looking at cognitive bias, which is a falsity in logic due to underlying experiences, attention, and many other things, it is not intentional. Logical fallacies are known to be somewhat intentional and often malicious. Below we have detailed some different types of logical fallacies to look out for.

**1. Slippery slope-** A slippery slope fallacy is best described as a hasty conclusion where someone equates an idea by skipping the steps in between to a final conclusion that could be a thousand steps away.

*Example: If we make a law that prohibits smoking on government property, then the government will ban cigarettes all together, making it illegal to smoke anywhere at any time.*

In this example, they jumped from a logical event to the worst case scenario, skipping all steps that would need to occur for landing at the end without cause.

**2. Hasty generalization-** A hasty generalization is reaching an ultimate conclusion based on your own personal bias and without fact or evidence to back it up.

*Example: Even though I've never met Sally, I can tell by her picture at the beach I won't like her.*

In this example, they prejudged Sally with personal bias without any evidence to back up their claim. Oftentimes, hasty generalization can lead to a missed opportunity, because you will put a negative thought on an opportunity before even giving it a chance.

**3. Post hoc ergo propter hoc:** This is a decision or conclusion decided upon by assuming that if the first situation occurred after the second, then the second must have caused the first.

*Example: I drank a bottle of soda, and now I have indigestion, so the soda must have caused it.*

In this example, they are blaming the soda for the indigestion without sufficient proof. The indigestion could have come from a number of things, but they have equated the first situation with the second.

**4. Genetic fallacy-** A genetic fallacy can be really bad at times. It is the belief that the origins of a person, an idea, an institute, or a theory determines the character, nature, or worth of that person, place, or thing.

*Example: The news article is a conservative publication, so you know whatever they print has to be true.*

In this example, they believed that because the publication shared their ideals, everything they printed was absolutely true. This goes against facts and logic.

**5. Circular argument-** A circular argument is simply

restating a claim instead of giving any back-up or factual evidence. They ignore any question being asked.

*Example: You should invite your aunt to the wedding because it would be mean to not invite her.*

In this example, the person basically said the same thing in two different ways.

**6. Either/or-** This type of logical fallacy over-simplifies a conversation by giving only two options (usually the best and the worst).

*Example: We either go on a diet or die from obesity.*

In this example, the person gave an ultimatum, basically. They completely left out the millions of other choices that sit between the two theories.

**7. Ad hominem-** An ad hominem is when, instead of giving their facts and evidence for a statement, a person hurls attacks at others.

*Example: Vegans struggle to get people on board with their cause because they are loud, obnoxious, and dirty hippies.*

In this example, they began the sentence by stating their concern or their topic of discussion but ended it with an attack instead of saying why they thought Vegans were struggling.

**8. Bandwagon-** The bandwagon fallacy is when a group

mentality is pushed onto a person in order to get them to believe what they believe.

*Example: If you truly believed in this country, you would let everyone, including children, own machine guns.*

In this example, the person is using the country as a whole group to get the other to believe in allowing children and citizens of the country to own machine guns.

**9. Red herring-** This is one of politics' greatest fallacies. Not only do politicians use it, but the supporters do as well. With so many issues being faced, it's hard not to accidentally slip into this fallacy on a regular basis.

*Example: I think what she wore is inappropriate, and the other party couldn't stop talking about my friend when they didn't like what she wore.*

In this example, instead of stating why they thought what she wore was inappropriate, they threw in a situation that was unrelated in an attempt to show cause, but not toward the initial person. They were dodging the original portion by stating something emotional afterward.

**10. Moral equivalence-** A moral equivalence is when minor infractions are compared to major ones, basically insinuating that they are both equally as immoral.

*Example: Anyone who supports gun rights hates children.*

At the beginning, this example shows the topic of contention but then skips over to a completely ridiculous statement trying to draw a rise out of the other person.

These are just some logical fallacies, and the list seems to grow on a daily basis. Now that we understand these, lets sink back into cognizant bias for a bit to understand the different types and how they affect mental modeling.

# Chapter Four: Types of Cognitive Bias

There are literally hundreds and even thousands of different types of cognitive bias, including some that we create ourselves in our own minds. However, switching from personal to business, we want to focus on recognizing these very common types of bias so that if you happen to find yourself in a similar situation, you are able to move through it. Having a hang-up in a business setting can land you in hot water. You want your work to be not only perfect, but thorough and thought-through. Our own cognitive bias can definitely get in the way of that.

Using mental models takes a lot of thought, a lot of work, and an understanding of the different situations that you will come across. Sometimes, if it's easier, if you find yourself stuck in any of the following bias types, you can switch up your mental model for something that will clear the system and get you running again. It all depends on you and your ability to surpass your own roadblocks. When it comes to cognitive bias, unfortunately, there is no one that can help you. You have to be able to spot these hang-ups before they take your project or your decision down the wrong path.

Some mental models will work out despite your use of bias in decision making, but that doesn't mean that the ultimate end goal shouldn't be to increase the quality of your work. If you are using mental modeling in your everyday life and you allow these biases to continue, then you are setting yourself up for a poor quality of life and a backup of these biases. By reinforcing them, you are telling your brain that you don't disagree, and, therefore, every time you come across a similar issue, decision, or project, you will find yourself in the same position.

## Types

Whether we are looking at confirmation bias or the heavy weighted anchor bias, they are all stop signs on your way to making a decision, choice, or setup for your projects. On a business level, these types of dilemmas aren't positive in any light. They will also recondition a team or staff to expect time delays in the future. Decisions in both your personal life and your career should be free of bias - or at least as free as you can possibly muster. Let's take a more in-depth look at some of the most common types of cognizant biases.

## The Ambiguity Effect

The ambiguity effect is something that we've all demonstrated once or twice in our lifetimes. It is the tendency to purposefully overlook the options that have a probability of positive outcomes as an unknown factor. Basically, we are picking the winners and not even attempting to take a chance on something that may or may not work out.

## Confirmation Bias

Confirmation bias happens when we tend to take new concepts we have recently come to understand and apply them to a belief we hold.

## Availability Heuristic

The availability heuristic refers to when someone comes to a conclusion based on the concepts and ideas that enter their mind immediately after thinking about a particular subject or topic.

## Halo Effect

The halo effect refers to when a person uses a subject to come up ideas about a completely different topic.

## Self-Serving Bias

The self-serving bias can be one of the most frustrating kinds to deal with. Someone who demonstrates this is very straight forward, upfront, and oftentimes loud and proud of everything that they do. When you have a self-serving bias, you tend to claim more of the responsibility of the successes and less of the failures. With this type of bias, it is also natural to see people interpret information in a way that is self-serving. This type of bias does not produce the kind of decision making, or project plan, in mental modeling that will be successful long term.

## Attentional Bias

This bias is a hiccup - an inability to fully engross yourself in the mental model - because of everything that is going on around you. Life is full of distractions, and your brain can't help but pull them in and process them. If you aren't careful, you could find yourself missing pertinent steps or options because your mind is not fully immersed within the information you should be processing. While multitasking can be a positive trait when it comes to hands-on projects, mental models require your full attention.

## Actor-Observer Bias

The actor-observer bias is a social bias that leads to long and overdrawn tendencies of explanation of other people's behavior to emphatically emphasize their positive personality and push down their influence on negative situations. It also works the opposite way when personality traits that are shown by others cause negative consequences but the situations are positive. This bias has a tendency to comingle with self-serving biases as well.

## Functional Fixedness

Functional fixedness bias is a behavior bias that creates a barrier of creativity for the person engaged in the mental model. Someone with a functional fixed bias has an inability to use an object in any other way than it is traditionally used. Within corporate settings, this can be a negative attribute since oftentimes creativity is the key to completing the work at hand. On a personal level, this will work against someone in situations such as budgeting, design, or even personal care.

## Anchoring Bias

The anchoring bias is much like the trait within mental models; it involves losing the ability to fully see the model in your head due to an anchor or one piece of information that is factual which has been presented. That one piece of information may create a personal or professional bias or a memory - something that you can't help but tether yourself to. This tether is going to affect your ability to fully see all of the options within your mental model.

## Misinformation Effect

The misinformation effect is a memory bias. It doesn't necessarily affect the creator on a regular basis, but it does create a less accurate memory of past events due to the interference of post-event information. In a work setting, this could be the last project finished. In a personal setting, it could refer to the events that happened the day before - This could include daydreaming about the date you had or the fight you experienced while attempting to keep your mind in a mental model.

## False Consensus Effect

The false consensus effect is a social bias that is often found among celebrities and even political heads. The false consensus bias leaves you with the tendency to overestimate how much others agree with you. This can lead to rash decisions being made based on a lack of input from others as well as an inability to fully listen to what they have to say. You may make decisions based on your own choices, having ingrained it in yourself that others are completely on the same page as you. This can lead to both professional and personal trouble, as well as a lack of understanding all of the options within your mental model.

## Optimism Bias

The optimism bias doesn't seem that bad at first glance, as someone with this bias has a tendency to be overly optimistic, happy, and always expecting a favorable and happy outcome. Unfortunately, when working on solving problems and making decisions, you have to be able to incorporate the negative aspects of information and actions. You must have the ability to weigh the pros and cons. Optimism bias can completely cloud you from taking risks, understanding risks, and catching errors before they destroy the plan created within your mental model.

## Automation Bias

The automation bias is incredibly important to focus on. We live in a world of apps, chats, project software, online lists, and the cloud. Even when you go to some grocery stores, all you have to do is pull up your phone number and all of your coupons are digitally available. The problem with digital reliance is the inability to think outside of the box. When you have a million-plus options for a decision, you need to be able to understand as many of those options as possible. The computer and digital world will only scratch the surface. You are a thinking, living, breathing person, while the computer communicates to you through a language of ones and zeroes, only answering the specific questions that you ask. When you have an automation bias, you are so reliant on those automated systems that you have a tendency to second guess your own creative mind. You may create a mental model in your head, but it's so much easier to press the delete button on the computer than to work through issues to get where you want to be.

## Courtesy Bias

Everyone grows up being taught to mind your manners, to avoid rocking the boat, to be pleasant, to be agreeable, and to work hard. Unfortunately, life is not that kind. When someone has a courtesy bias, they tend to tone down their options and decisions to make them more socially correct. This keeps them from finding those hard and possibly even controversial answers to and options for their mental model. Rocking the boat is something you should strive to do. There is far too much kindness in the world already, and though you don't want to be a tyrant, your job is to create and decide. Those two things need an honest mind and an honest answer.

These are just the tip of the iceberg when it comes to cognizant bias. There are so many other things that create a rift between you and your mental model. If used correctly, the mental model can open up many doors for your career and your life as a whole. Understanding the major players in biased thoughts will prepare you to key your eye out for them, understand them, and above all, avoid them in any way that you can.

Mental models, as discussed earlier in this book, can cover every part of your life. Productivity, problem solving, and decision making are actions that you have to take almost every day. To do this, you need to have a thorough understanding of what the issue is and of the model that fits it perfectly. That way, before you even lift a finger to begin the project, you've mapped it out in your head so clearly that there was no doubt that you were on the right track.

In the following chapter, we will dive further into the world of mental modeling. We will discuss the most famous mental models and where they stand within the productive realm of problem solving. Additionally, we will discuss the people behind the models, showing that mental models aren't just for the everyday person; they have been used to make millions of dollars for people.

# Chapter Five: Mental Models for Productivity, Problem Solving, and Decision Making

In Chapter Five, we're going to take a good look at productivity, problem solving, decision making, and the most successful mental models in history under each of those categories. Everything that you learn and everything that you do concerning mental models revolves around productivity, problem solving, and decision making. They are the three main factors in everyday life.

In general terms, productivity is defined by the Business Dictionary as "a measure of the efficiency of a person, machine, factory, system, etc., in converting inputs into useful outputs". When a company or an individual calculates that they have a higher productivity, that means they are accomplishing more without utilizing any extra resources. In the broad sense of the term, productivity is the act of transforming physical and human resources into needed or desired outputs. Productivity always correlates with an increase in quality of work, quality of life, and quality as a whole for society. We will be discussing the best practices for productivity in Chapter Six.

Problem solving goes hand in hand with productivity. It won't be very often that you have an extremely productive day without facing some sort of problem. These issues can be easily tackled by implementing your mental models. ASQ defines problem solving as the physical act of defining the problem, figuring out the cause, pinpointing it specifically, deciding on a solution to the problem, and implementing that decision.

In order to effectively get through life, work, and your family life, you must learn how to successfully implement problem solving techniques. Not all problems will require a full-scale mental model, but by the end of the book, you will be able to quickly figure out which will be the best method to use. However, if the problem doesn't warrant an all-out mental model, there is a very simplified version that you can take advantage of, often within seconds.

**Define the problem-** You want to first figure out what is fact and what are opinions within the problem. You have to be thorough, even if you are quick to point out the exact underlying causes of the issue. Look for information about those causes, gather facts, and understand what the issue is completely. You should state the problem back to yourself, decide what standard it needs to be at, and only when all the information is collected should you move on to the next step.

**Generate alternative solutions-** Don't just go with the first thing that pops into your head unless, of course, it is an emergency situation where a quick response time is needed. Brainstorm ideas, flipping through your third eye, noting every possibility you can to fix it.

**Evaluate and select-** Pull all of the bias you have out of the situation and evaluate your options. Then choose your course of action.

**Implement-** Move to implement a solution. This is the point in which you can really shine as a leader. Whether it is at work or in front of your children, understanding, evaluating, and implementing a solution in a calm manner will show them you have everything under control.

This small mental model can be used on a larger scale if necessary, but it comes in handy when you have but a few quick moments to decide upon the solution. You always want to have a process, though, even if it is unseen by anyone but yourself. Doing things in a manufactured and structured way will result in positive outcomes.

The third action is decision making. Most likely, while you were problem solving and while you were working through your productivity, you were also making decisions. We make choices on a daily basis that we don't even recognize doing. When it comes to the big ones, both personally and professionally, it is ideal to understand the process. Fortunately, the seven steps of decision making are almost identical to that of problem solving.

- Identify what decision to mak.e

- Gather all the information about the choices.

- Figure out what the alternatives are.

- Weigh the information and evidence you've been given.

- Select your decision based on evidence.

- Make your final decision.

- Review that decision when it's complete, and make sure you understand the consequences.

Once you have a firm grasp on these actions, you can then move on to the most popular and lucrative mental models ever used.

# Productivity

The first of the popular mental models falls under the productivity category. These practices are to help you move to a better and more productive day. When you have to work through problems, issues, and decisions, it can get overwhelming. Sometimes, the information can be so dense that your brain struggles to pull the important factors up into your mental model. If possible, go slow so that you are able to tackle the day with fervor and knowledge.

## Pareto Principle

The Pareto principle is also known as the 80/20 rule, the law of the vital few, and the principle of factor sparsity. Ultimately, the rule states that for 80 percent of the effort exerted, you will see 20 percent results. In 1920, Vilfedo Pareto made note of the 80/20 rule, but it wasn't until much later that the management consultant, Joseph M. Juran, suggested the principle. He then subsequently named it after Pareto. Pareto's notation of the rule came when he showed that 80 percent of Italian land was owned by only 20 percent of the population.

If you take this theory and convert it to business, it is said that 80 percent of the sales of a company come from 20 percent of the clients. It was initially used as an example of the distribution of wealth among the population. From there, it grew to cover all areas of study, including math, economics, and, for our purposes, the mental model for productivity.

This principle is translated into a mental model for the use of searching for answers. Facts and information are a vital part of working through any mental model. To be more productive, you are simply searching for the vital few in the vast landscape of the trivial many. As was discussed in previous chapters, information is almost infinite and might as well be when compared to how much our brains can hold. When searching for the specific information you need, you have to push aside the noise and find the vital few pieces that will help you work through your mental model.

During his time studying, then referred to as the 80/20 rule, Pareto performed several small experiments. Those experiments were then adjusted to evolve with the times. Here are several things you can do while implementing the Pareto principle as your mental model:

1. Skim through the multitude of articles online, choosing the two best ones to fully read through.

2. Rank your to-do list according to efforts and results so that you are prioritizing your actions.

3. Organization can be key. Go through your emails and

begin grouping them into basic categories. For those that you find yourself typing over and over again, use canned responses, eliminating time spent in the future.

4. Use an 80/20 template to grade your personal productivity. Self-analyze with a timed tracker in order to find what is productive out of your activities versus those distractions we don't always catch onto unless we literally write them down.

These tasks can be completed for general improvement of productivity and for specific marked tasks. If you have a large project to work on, you can use this productivity mental model in order to get yourself on the right track, to clear away unneeded distractions within a workflow, and to minimize your outgoing tasks to those that bring the largest results.

## The 2-Minute Rule

The 2-minute rule is the perfect way to move on from a task you are using simply to procrastinate. David Allen explained the rule in simple terms. It  states that when a new habit begins, you should make sure that it takes less than two minutes to complete.

You're probably thinking that sounds impossible. It can take two minutes just to get organized, but that is merely a frame of mind. Nearly all habits can be scaled down and turned into a two-minute version of itself. For example, reading a half of a book before bed at night can easily become reading one page before going to sleep. Putting on your schedule to meditate for thirty minutes a day knowing you'll probably not get to i may become a two-minute meditation. Anyone can do anything for two minutes, and oftentimes, when you start it and find that it is productive, you are already in the motion to complete it.

For example, not too many people actually enjoy working out. It usually seems like a fantastic idea until you have to do it. However, if you tell yourself that instead of running for thirty minutes, you will start by tying your shoes, it will be easier to move forward into tackling the entire thirty minutes of running in two-minute increments. One goal completed leads into another and then another. These small two-minute goals are called "gateway habits". You can also use the gateway habits to begin solving problems that seem too overwhelming to tackle.

This brings us to the next set of mental models, which are used to solve our toughest problems.

# Problem Solving

Problem solving is one of those things that we do a million times a day without even realizing it. It's only when the very tough problems arise that we begin to stress out. However, just like every other process, there is a mental model that can help you through this. The first of those is the inversion mental model. It's a model that can be used alone or that can be combined with other models through your problem solving process.

## Inversion Mental Model

The inversion mental model, though listed under the problem solving category, is actually one of the most powerful tools in the mental model toolbox. The inversion method blossomed from the mathematical elements of German mathematician Carl Gustav Jacob Jacobi, who worked on elliptical functions. He would solve his problems with the following strategy: man muss immer umkehren. This means "invert, always invert."

From that thought sprung the inversion mental model used to show that you can't just look at your problems in one manner. In order to get the entire scope of a project, you have to look at it forward and backward. When you invert someone, it forces your mind to see it in a different light and to uncover truths about the problem or project you have at hand. Obviously, thinking about the exact opposite of the problem doesn't really come naturally to us, but some of the most brilliant people in history have solved problems doing just that.

Don't expect to always invert your problems and magically find the answers; it doesn't quite work like that. What it will do is give you another perspective to draw from, which will allow you to see problematic areas as well as clues toward the path you need to take in order to break through those problems.


## Occam's Razor


Simply put, Occam's razor says that the simplest of answers is always the correct answer. We need to stop racking our brains attempting to find complex solutions to problems and begin focusing on what actually works for it. This mental model is great for solving problems, but it is also good for drawing initial conclusions before the bulk of the facts or before certain information is brought into the picture.

Arthur Conan Doyle's, "Sherlock Holmes", explained Occam's razor. He asserted that if you get rid of the impossible, the thing that remains - no matter how ridiculous, impossible, or even improbable - must be the truth.

Scientifically, there have been studies that have proven the theory of Occam's razor. The principle of minimum energy, a sector of the second law of thermodynamics, simply finds that whenever it's possible, the least amount of energy is used. This concept is utilized in science, business, project management, problem solving, and many more fields.

William of Ockham, a friar, philosopher, and theologian in the 14th century, didn't exactly theorize Occam's razor, but he was known for deducing, which helped the other writers develop the model. It is used across the board to prove or disprove specific theories. Below are some examples of how Occam's razor has been used in the past.

**Religion-** The model has been used to attempt to prove or disprove the existence of God.

**Scientific theories-** Scientists use the model to decide whether a hypothesis is genuinely purposeful. If it is easy to be proven or falsified, this is usually a good start. The more complex the hypothesis is, the denser the facts have to become to justify the theory.

**Medicine-** Doctors use Occam's razor every time they see a patient. They attempt to find the fewest causes for multiple symptoms and the most likely cause of their ailment.

As with any model, always keep in mind that they are not 100 hundred percent fool-proof. That is why it is a process - a discovery through facts and theories - to find the correct answer. Always draw the conclusions you believe will fit best with the situation, and never be afraid to discredit the model if it doesn't fit in with the project at hand.

Now, let's move on to the last but most exciting set of models for decision making.

## Decision Making

Decisions, decisions, decisions. There are always so many decisions to make. At the end of the day, your ultimate decision will be the end of that mental model, most likely. Whether it's a decision based on an action, a course of action, or an issue you have been mulling over, mental models can help you sort it out, push any emotions to the side, and create a solid list of options from which to draw your conclusions.

### Warren Buffett and the Circle of Competence

Before we jump into the plethora of mental models that Warren Buffet swears by, let's take a look at who he is. Born on August 30th, 1930, Warren Buffet started out living a normal life in Omaha, Nebraska. He was the second oldest of three children and the son of Congressman Howard Buffett. He began his early childhood education like anyone else, attending Rose Hill Elementary, but in 1942, after his father was elected to his first of many terms in the United States Congress, he and his family moved to Washington, DC. Buffett finished out elementary and middle school there, going on to graduate from Woodrow Wilson High School in 1947.

Initially, due to his success with small entrepreneurial jobs and minor investments, Buffett didn't find the need to go to college. However, his father being who he was insisted that he attend. Business was in Buffett's blood; he caught the fever at just seven years old after reading "One Thousand Ways to Make $1000", a book he borrowed from the library. Warren Buffett hit the ground running after that, selling gum, Coke bottles, and weekly magazines on foot door-to-door.

He didn't stop there. Throughout high school, he delivered newspapers, sold stamps and golf balls, and detailed cars for money. In his sophomore year, he and a friend invested $25 to buy a pinball machine that they put in the local barber shop. In less than a year, they owned several machines in different barber shops across Omaha. This was Buffett's first business sale. He and his friend sold the pinball business to a war veteran for $1,200.

By the time Buffett had finished college, he had invested in the stock market, worked at farms, bought land, and had close to $10,000 in his savings account. At the end of his collegiate years, Buffett had earned a Bachelor of Science in Business Administration from the University of Nebraska and a Masters of Science in Economics from Columbia, but he was just getting warmed up.

Throughout the years, Buffett began acquiring partnerships under Buffett Partnership Ltd. By 1960, just as he met his future partner, Charlie Munger, he was operating seven partnerships and found eleven doctors willing to invest with him in the Sanborn Map Company. Eventually, after that success, he would go on to purchase almost 25 percent of the company. Two years later, he found himself with a fifty percent return on his investment.

In 1962, Buffett officially became a millionaire. He took all of his partnerships, merged them together, and invested in a textile company he would eventually take control of. Berkshire Hathaway eventually moved from textiles into insurance, closing down all of the factories. Through the years, he invested in private companies, gained a 25 percent ownership in ABC media, and eventually bought 7 percent of the Coca-Cola Company's stock for 1.02 billion dollars, which was his most fruitful investment.

He officially became a billionaire in 1990 when Berkshire Hathaway began selling class A shares at $7,175 each. Through the following years, he would join forces with AIG during their biggest scandals, enter into contracts with the government, making $2 billion dollars from the deal, and eventually begin giving out 85 percent of Berkshire Hathaway's holdings to different foundations, the largest being the Bill and Melinda Gates Foundation.

From there, he invested in companies like IBM, raising their stocks higher than they had seen in years. After the recession and a poor investment in oil, Buffett was able to bring Berkshire Hathaway back up, making over six billion dollars in net profits. Even with the tumultuous scandals, the housing crisis, and the influx of money from his days of delivering newspapers, Buffett stayed grounded. During a presentation at Georgetown University in 2013, he likened the US government to a bank, admitting that they were generating 80 to 90 billion dollars a year. However, wealth equality was on his mind.

In an article Buffett wrote in Bloomberg in 2013, he expressed his concern for equality of finances by explaining that we have learned the basis of selling and producing goods, but we haven't learned how to share that money and that success. He felt that it was an obligation, not a choice, for a society of such fruitfulness, to make sure that no one gets left too far behind.

So, what was the key to Buffett's success? Well, it's probably not just one single thing, but he has spoken numerous times about the power of mental models. Below we have detailed some of the most poignant ones he used throughout the years.

## Circle of Competence

The circle of competence is not a complicated model in the least. It states that some people have acquired a bank of useful knowledge in certain areas of the world through experience or study. Some of these areas are understandable by most everyone while others require a specialty. Buffett believes that you don't necessarily need all the knowledge of a specialist to invest in the more complicated fields. What you do want to do is have a very good grasp on what you are knowledgeable about and stick to that circle. The circle will widen, though slowly.

Buffett explained the circle of competence of one of his business managers by explaining that he could not have given one of his managers $200 million worth of Berkshire Hathaway stock when he bought it. It would have been pointless because she didn't understand stock. What she did understand was cash, furniture, and real estate. He explained that if you were going to work with "Mrs. B" inside of her own circle of confidence, then you would expect her to buy 5,000 end tables if the price were right. You would expect her to buy twenty carpets in odd lots because she understands carpet. He finishes the explanation by relaying that core message that even if General Motors' stock was 50 cents per share, she would never buy because she doesn't have stocks in her inner circle.

This represents how Mrs. B stayed safe within her circle of competence. Could she possibly have made more edging away from it? Possibly, but it was a definite for a secure future if she stayed inside of it.

However, the circle of competence doesn't just apply to business and investments, but covers every aspect of your life. And if you want to improve that life find your circle of competence and operate within its walls. One of Buffett's other well known mental models was the 2-List Strategy.

## 2-List Strategy

Warren Buffett liked to help other people find their footing in the world of finance and business. So, he created what was eventually called the 2-list strategy. The strategy had three simple steps that anyone could do at any point. Below are the three steps.

1. **List your top 25 lifetime goals**- Take as long as you need to create the list, but make sure you put them in the order by which you are most passionate about them.

2. **Choose the five most important goals**- Imagine that you were given the rule that you would only be able to accomplish five of those twenty five goals; pick those out.

3. **Create two lists**- Put your most important on one sheet, and the other twenty on the opposite sheet of paper. Warren explained that while the list of twenty things might seem important, they are to be forgotten, not touched, and filed away for later. The five things that were most important to you should be your focus. You cannot take on anything else until those five goals are accomplished.

By creating a separation, you are focusing your attention on five goals. With twenty five, there is no way that you could keep up, but with the twenty still looming in the background calling for you, it should motivate you to work harder and faster on the list of five you still have in hand. Buffett is convinced that prioritizing your life and focusing on the major goals is imperative for success. If you reach all twenty five, that's great and you can make a new list, but focus on just five of them at a time.

## 10/10/10 Method

The 10/10/10 method wasn't spoken about by Buffett or Munger, but it falls along the same lines as the other methods they speak about on a regular basis. This method is very simple and could help you from jumping into decisions without thoroughly thinking them through. The premise is easy - when you are conflicted about a decision or an action to be taken, you should stop and ask yourself the following three questions:

- How will I feel about it in 10 minutes?

- How will I feel about it in 10 months?

- How will I feel about it in 10 years?

As Zat Rana put it in his Medium article entitled "The 10/10/10 Method: Make Decisions Like Warren Buffett and Ray Dalio", "The quality of your daily decisions informs the quality of your life." No matter where those decisions come from, whether it be work, home, dreams of the future, they all demand a place in where you end up. By using the 10/10/10 method, you are ensuring that you are doing your best to be conscious about your today so that tomorrow will look like the future you dreamed of. Even within the office, you can use this method, making decisions for your company or with your company to decide on its future in business.

## Attribution Theory

The attribution theory is also called the "cause theory". This theory, stated by the Florida International University, finds that if you can affect the way that people understand what is happening in your company right now, then you can possibly influence how they behave in the future. This is an extremely important aspect of business and has the possibility of stabilizing your company far into the future.

With that being said, the attribution theory can also be used in your home life. If you are raising children and want them to grow up to be strong and successful, you can implement the same practices. Be honest and open with them, listen to them, and make sure they understand what is happening in the here and now. When you do this, you will be able to shift their fate in the future.

The theories and models discussed in this chapter only begin to scratch the surface of what is out there. By using Buffett and Munger as two prominent examples of the power of mental models, you can begin to see how important they are to your life and business. Begin to take in the information of these models - try them out, play around with it. Eventually, you will see that there is nothing that can't be accomplished if you put your mind to it, clear your space, and allow the answers to evolve from your own knowledge.

Now that we are aware of the ways to use the mental models and avoid the bias traps we all tend to fall into, let's take a look at some of the best and worst practices when it comes to productivity, problem solving, and decision making.

# Chapter Six: Best Practices and What to Avoid

Everyone wants to be successful. Whether its owning your own business, raising a healthy and thriving family, or climbing the corporate ladder, barely anyone settles for mediocre. There are certain traits that all successful businesspeople tend to have, but unlike popular belief, they weren't born with them, but rather they are learned. The top executives around the country started out practicing the best tactics for their careers and, for most, it paid off. The important thing to remember is that when you reach the top, you shouldn't stop implementing those practices. There is always somewhere else to grow your motivation, even if it's outside of the workplace.

To set you up for a bright and exciting future, let's review the best practices and which ones to avoid. Most of these tips are ones that you can begin right away with no practice needed.

> *There is an enormous lie underlying business, the lie that decisions are made rationally, applying logic and expertise, sifting evidence, and carefully weighing alternatives. However, the science is clear: in general, we don't really make decisions that way - we fake it, instead. Boyd, (2017).*

At the heart of business, executives are admitting to making choices for their companies with little to no thought about it. There is no mental methodology, no research, no sweat, and no anxiety. They are simply dropping the ball. However, a 2017 study by Bain researches found that those decisions correlated strongly with the financial performance of the company.

Now, we aren't all executives. We aren't all top ten in the company, nor do we own huge conglomerates with millions and billions of dollars to throw around, but the practices we implement are the same that the top level executives should be. When you show your best side from the bottom up, there is a learning process that occurs. You understand the importance of the implementation of best practices, and you also know the danger of those practices that should be avoided at all costs. Whether you learn through reading about them or through painful trial and error, they are processes you want to steer clear of.

Keeping with the major theme in both life and in business, we are going to continue on with our focus centered around productivity, problem solving, and decision making. These are the three vital processes that you can't get around, but they can make or break your choices and decisions. Now that you understand the mental model, the bias, and the lucrative practice of implementing these tactics in your life and business, let's talk about some best practices that you can easily do on a daily basis, as well as some practices to strictly avoid.

## Best Practices for Success

Everyone wants to be successful. Whether its owning your own business, raising a healthy and thriving family, or climbing the corporate ladder, barely anyone settles for mediocre. There are certain traits that all successful businesspeople tend to have, but unlike popular belief, they weren't born with them, they are learned. The top executives around the country started out practicing the best tactics for their careers and for most, it paid off. The important thing to remember is that when you reach the top, you don't stop implementing those practices. There is always somewhere else to grow your motivation, even if its outside of the workplace.

To set you up for a bright and exciting future, lets review the best practices, and those to avoid. Most of these tips are ones that you can begin right away, no practice needed.

# Productivity

You may have an office next to someone that always seems on the go, on top of their work, and ready for the next assignment. They get so much accomplished in one day you wonder if they are even human. But don't worry, the guy three doors down is not secretly Superman, he's just mastered some really simple habits that can completely change your productivity levels. All you have to do is take it step by step, implement them, and then watch your productivity soar.

## Messy Desk, Messy Mind

Sure, we've all seen the scene in the movie where the brilliant artist sits amongst hundreds of stacked canvases, ashtrays overflowing with cigarette ashes, his hair wild and his clothes either far too dirty for human wear, or just made like that because he's a dark brooding artist. But hey, get your head out of the oil paints, that is not real life, at least not for those of us who have bosses, tight schedules, and a small desk to get all of the work done from.

One of the first things that you need to do in order to declutter your productivity, is to declutter your workspace. Mugs on mugs upon mugs of stale coffee cups, papers everywhere, an old apple core from two months before completely dried out on a stack of papers you aren't really sure are yours...that's not going to help you become productive. Have you ever spent the day cleaning your house? You scrub and declutter, and clean, and when you're finished, you just feel so much better. So relaxed and calm, so ready to tackle the world. It's no different with your desk.

You are already working from a space that isn't your home, so comfort isn't optimal. When you begin to organize your papers, dispose of trash, compile your notes in the cloud, and fill out that calendar you've had on the desk for 6 months, you are going to be able to have a full grasp on what you need to accomplish. Tasks won't take you so long. You won't have to search through stacks of papers and banana peels to find the notes you need. Those mental models will actually be helpful.

## 90-Minute Power Work

Some days are just a bore at the office. It's raining out the window, your boss is in a bad mood, and Cindy has a cold, the tissues beginning to pile up like an avalanche of plague and snot. Your attention wavers from office emails to your social media page. You stare at the clock, counting down the glacially paced minutes until you can finally grab your coat and run, not walk to your car. But what about that is productive? Okay, we all get it, you can't be energizer on the go every day. Warren Buffett probably took days off too when he was starting out. Okay, maybe not, but nonetheless, you are human and allowed to have those days. But to make sure, that even on those days, you are getting something accomplished, set out 90 minutes of time in your eight hour workday to go as hard as you possibly can.

Don't look back, don't answer the phone, ignore the creature Cindy has turned into as it creeps down the hall hacking up a lung, and just work. Oftentimes you'll find that once you get going, nothing is going to stop you. So, your 90 minute power work session might have started off as a struggle, you're now blasting through your work, with everyone else scowling as they walk past your office. Bad days are gumption traps but those traps were made to be broken, and to be honest, they break pretty easy.

Progress is progress, but remember those five goals you set aside with Mr. Buffett. They aren't going to be met if you sit there staring off into space. Give the 90-minute power work session a chance. And if you find yourself rolling through, don't stop.

## Why Overwork Yourself?

Okay yeah, we've all heard the cliché story of the billionaire who worked seven days a week, slept at his office, and that's what it took to make his fortune. That stinks. While goals are important, what's the point of having them if you're just going to work yourself into the ground over them? You have to be smart about it. Stanford professor, John Pencavel did a study based on the labor hours during World War I. People then were working around the clock trying to produce for the war and for the people there at home.

What Pencavel found, though, was that output was pretty proportionate to the amount of time they worked...up to 49 hours. After that, the productivity took a nosedive. Someone working 70 hours a week during that period put in the same productivity as someone who worked just 56 hours. There is something called getting burnt out. How are you supposed to come up with brilliant ideas for your goals if you walk around like a zombie?

The bottom line is, don't overwork yourself. It's one thing to volunteer to get yourself noticed, but another to do it because you think it will help your goals. Again, what good are goals if you're just a skeleton in the corner of your office when they finally come to fruition. Slow down there, buddy, take a deep breath and do what you know you can handle.

## Efficiency

Efficiency and productivity go hand in hand. When you slow down on tasks that are either hard for you, or are boring to you, it impedes your entire flow. You were just doing so good and now your downing coffee, falling asleep as you fix the millionth paper from the home office.

If you can, delegate the responsibilities that you struggle with to someone else on the team. I you aren't in a position to delegate, do what's best for you. Some people thrive on knocking out all of the little boring stuff first, while others knock out the heavy stuff and relax as they barely pay attention to the tasks they dislike. Either way keep moving. If you find something weighing you down, stop. Move to something else because that one assignment could ruin your entire pace.

## ZZZZZ

The University of Michigan did a study that found taking a daytime nap decreased impulsive actions and boosted tolerance for anxiety and frustration. Of course, they probably didn't take into account the whole sleeping on the job thing. While I wouldn't suggest requesting nap time if you are a construction worker, road worker, or any other dangerous job, if you have a desk then consider bringing it up to them. Of course, don't be shocked if they laugh wildly at you and close the door again. It was worth a try, right?

Speaking of sleep, you're not going to get anything done if you don't get a full night's rest. Your mind will be sluggish, your temperament off, and attempting your mental models will be more than a challenge. The average adult needs 7.7 hours of sleep a night to keep a healthy immune, cardiovascular, and weight system in place. That sleep also helps with cognitive function and focus.

## Food and Exercise

Just as sleep is vital to your health, so is nutritious food and physical activity. Whether it's a walk in the morning or a full on workout after a long day at the office, getting up and really moving your body will do wonders for your brain. Physical activity has shown to improve cognitive health, memory, and physical conditioning. With a good nutritious meal plan, you will be perked and ready to go each morning. Exercise also helps with sleep, allowing your body to fully recover overnight. Fasting, for some, has shown to also improve cognitive function as well as improve energy and control the metabolism. All of these things are important regardless of your professional life, but will help to show improvement in your quality of work as well.

# Problem Solving Best Practices

From the spat you broke up between your children earlier in the morning, to the project that is looming over your head at work, we use our problem solving skills on a regular basis. This world is made up of an array of different people and it is not crazy to think that we would all need to have some basic problem solving skills. Children learn these skills when they are just toddlers, advancing forward on two feet, exploring the world around them without holding mommy or daddy's hand. We naturally develop problem solving skills, though some aren't as strong as others. In order to grow better at this tool, there are several best practices you can follow.

## Systems

I know you've probably heard the word systems about nine hundred times, especially if you work in a traditional corporate career, but there is definitely a reason for that. As problem solving, decision making, bright eyed employees, it's vital to have control over our ability to be creative, but creative doesn't mean chaos. A systematic approach that is in line with your workplace or home conditions and constraints will really assist you in moving forward in the process.

Let's face it, stressing out over problems is already hard enough but to add chaos to the mix is asking for trouble. Maintain a structured environment and approach to your job and you will find it helps with organization and focus as well. No matter the situation, find a system to compliment it. Systems are the key to an organized, functional work and home spaces. It's already crazy enough out there in this world, don't make it any harder on yourself.

## Turn That Frown Upside Down

When a problem does come up, stop what you are doing for a moment and remember that with every problem comes a lesson. Instead of getting irritated and frustrated with the problems, view them as opportunities for a better and more knowledgeable self. Oftentimes you will find that problems become life changing events, especially when it comes to the brain and how you perceive the world around you. Make the most of every situation, no matter how hard it may seem.

## Perspective

Perspective can be the difference between stress and anger and an understanding of others views and sides. Changing your perspective on things allows you to see a little bit better into the world around you. There are always a multitude of ways to solve a problem, but if you feel like nothing else is working, begin to change your own mindset. You may also want to seek advice or time with a psychologist to discuss the other troubles you have.

Sometimes taking a break from the situation can help tremendously. Being over run is not fun, and add trying to cook, take care of the kids, and take care of your significant other. Oftentimes, that small hour break brought me back to my current place in life with a renewed and refreshed ability to handle any problem sent my way. All it took was a change in my own perspective.

## Evaluation

While I understand that we, as part of this society, receive more than enough evaluations through our lives, this is about you evaluating yourself. Let's face it, we aren't always master at our own success. We go through the motions, finding ourselves bottlenecked in a situation or issue. When this happens, it continues to pull and tug at our irritation and lack of focus. Sometimes stepping back and reevaluating our processes can help to unlock that kink in our creative nature.

Even in the times you aren't struggling with a cramped brain or a brick wall, evaluating and starting fresh on a regular basis is an amazing way to bring vitality back into your personal and professional life. Evaluations don't have to be professional, but you have to have a thorough idea in your head what conditions you work best in. That way when you are changing your processes, you change them for the better.

## Decision Making Best Practices

Imagine this. Everyone in your life, moving and milling, pushing, and attentive to the decisions that had to be made throughout the day. That would be a beautiful thing, but unfortunately, that isn't something that actually happens. Decision making can be stressful, but it's necessary in the world of business, just as its necessary at home. Try not to take on the entire load on your own but if you do have to, know that you are equipped with the tools you will need to find the best path for the decision you have to make.

On top of the mental models, decisions need to spread wide, encompassing everyone as a team and as individuals. In order for this process to go smoothly, there are several best practices that decision makers can follow to take some of the stress off of their shoulders.

## Too Many Bosses but No Decisions

This situation is almost inevitable. Whether you are working on a group project at the office, or you go home to your bossy two year old, giving you "the look" as she spews out her jumbled speech like she was your mother, you have to begin to take everything in stride. In a perfect world everyone would just let you roll right through the decision making processes, everything left up to you. But sadly, that is not how it goes. What you can do is make sure there are as few hands in the project as possible to avoid confusion.

## Training

If you are in a position to be the person that directs the training of staff in your work environment, make sure that you are really heavily focusing on a culture of decision and problem solving mindsets. These types of professional development programs ensures that you and your staff are ready and equipped to handle any issues if they should come up. Some of the most important aspects of the work mind, to instill in everyone, would be to know your cognitive biases and push through them, make clear and concise decisions when it comes to everything in your life. Always have processes and strategies written out before you even begin the training so that everyone is capable of following along. Ultimately, by the end of this book you will be taking the reins, looking to push harder and faster through everything.

## Checklists

With projects looming, children screaming every morning over the first cup of coffee for the day, and the disheartening number of things on the to-do list, you may be feeling pretty irritated. Checklists may sound boring and obtuse, but they are still a brilliant way of documenting the things you needed to accomplish, and keep it all in a tight, neat circle without chaos ensuing. Not only that, but these checklists enable you to pull those cognitive biases right out of your head.

Harvard Business Review, speaking about the glory of checklists, quoted Cloverpop when they discussed the steps and tools you could use when getting a story or project off of the ground. The following steps by Cloverpop symbolize the freedom to do this not only professionally but privately.

1. First you jot down five already existing company goals that will be impacted by the decision. If you focus your mind on the important things, you will avoid making up reasons for your decision.

2. Brainstorm and write down four or more, alternatives.

The alternatives should be realistic, and may actually take some real effort and creative thought processes. Expanding your choices improves your decision making leaps and bounds.

3. Figure out what the most important information is, and write down the parts that you are missing. You want to avoid ignoring the unknowns and focusing solely on the known.

4. Create a brief, thought out story of what you expect that decision's impact will have a year down the road. This will help you think of similar experiences and give you a broader perspective.

5. Bring a team of less than six stakeholders into the process. You want to reduce your own biases.

6. You want to document the final decision, why it was made, and how many of the team are in support of it. This creates a commitment as well as a base to measure your results from.

7. Have a follow-up on that decision in a couple of months. You don't want to forget to check in on whether the decision was working or not. If not this will allow you to make corrections, and take those findings into fact for future decision making processes.

These tools, coupled with the mental models you have learned, will assist you in your journey for a better you, and for better processes throughout your entire project journey. However, understanding what the project entails and using best practices aren't the only thing you have to take care of when you go into a meeting. You also have to know what you need to do to be able to sell them on this structured environment.

Here is a list of things that you should avoid at all costs when it comes to productivity.

## What to Avoid

This book has been all about the things you need to do to implement your mental model and get wild crazy in your new lifestyle. However, with every good comes some sort of bad. There are a ton of things that can affect your productivity, your problem solving abilities, and your decision making skills. Luckily, most of them are very simple and very easy to fix. If you are going to put out the effort to change your life for the better, you should do it from the floor to the ceiling.

Below we will discuss the different avenues you should avoid when you are implementing best practices and preparing for your new life. Make sure to take note of these, because you may have to switch up different routines and plans in order to keep the negativity and irritation down.

## Productivity

Let's face it, there is nothing worse in this world then setting yourself up for a productive day and getting sideswiped by something you didn't even realize could knock you out of whack. Being productive day after day can get daunting, and there are several things that can make it even harder to get through.

## Planning

You've got your clean workspace, you slept the night before, you worked out and ate a healthy breakfast, and now you're ready to tackle the day. But wait...what was it that you were supposed to do again?

Planning is one of the most instrumental parts of being productive. You wouldn't plan a trip across the country without knowing your way, so why would you start your day without a roadmap to the tasks and jobs you had to complete. When we don't plan, we end up teetering back and forth, trying to figure out what needs to be done first and what can wait. That alone cuts your productivity by huge amounts. Always sit down the day before and plan out your next day's tasks so you can complete all the tasks you needed to, without wasting time trying to figure out what they are.

## Multitasking

While in the thick of it, adrenalin running high, pushing through the controlled chaos, multitasking can be a life saver. However, on a normal day, it can be one of the biggest threats to your productivity. Research has shown that people who constantly multitask throughout the day drop in their productivity levels by forty percent. They also take twice as long to finish a task, and make twice as many errors. Pick up one project, one task at a time and work it from beginning to end. You will really understand the importance of this when your checklists begins to disappear.

## Yes! Yes! Yes!

How about...no. One habit that many people struggle with is the inability to tell someone no when they are asked to take on more work. The need to please the upper management seems lost when the word no comes out of your mouth. But guess what, always saying yes, and then having too much to do, can result in sub-par work. On top of that you become exhausted, burnt out, and irritable. All of these things can inhibit you from successfully completing mental models and spiral your entire day. At that point, productivity goes right out of the window.

Start to learn that it's okay to say no. In fact, the majority of your bosses won't even bat an eyelash at it. Assertiveness and taking care of yourself needs to be a priority in your life. If you are exhausted, running around multitasking, with no real plan in place, your problem solving skills will be useless.

## Problem Solving

Solution finding is a necessary skill in order to navigate the project, the process, and the people around you. With bias working against you, the best thing you can do is follow all of the best practices, and then stay as far as you can out of the possible inhibitors to your problem solving processes. Below are the top four things you should avoid when you are problem solving.

## The Voices Are All Wrong

Solving problems can become more complex than just running over the facts and making the best possible assessment. Sometimes you need a team of people to make these decisions. When you don't involve the right people in your conversations, you are setting back your ability to solve whatever problem they are facing. Always make sure to do a thorough investigation of the issue and bring in the best people to help you find what you're looking for.

## One Step Behind

It's hard to solve a problem when the other people involved aren't anywhere close to being on the same page. Just because you see something as a problem, doesn't mean that everyone else will. It's vital to keep the project team on the same page with everything. That way they all know where the group stands and you aren't stuck switching up your game play because you had a different expectation from the meeting. This can happen to anyone, so if you see that confused face, reach out and pull them back in, you'll be glad you did later on down the road.

## Fixing the Pipes When the Window is the Problem

When large projects become a source of issue, you immediately spring into action, trying to find the source of the problem. Too often you end up discussing this with the team or a fellow coworker. Sometimes in those conversations you can get off track with your thoughts and end up rattling off a list of issues with the project. However, before you go swooping in with your magic wand, you want to make sure that the thing you're fixing is actually going to make the problem any better. There is nothing wrong with listing the possible flaws, but fix the source of the issues first and then you can attack the little ones.

## Missing the Framework

Solutions begin with structured problem solving skills. When a problem arises you should immediately take notice of what sector of the company is in charge of that area, and then go to those specialists to analyze the issue. There are five questions that help you avoid this altogether.

- What problem are we trying to solve?

- Why is this an issue?

- What are we currently doing to address this problem?

- What could we do differently/better?

- How can we move these ideas forward? What are the next steps?

Make sure to pay close attention to the flaws, slips, and the unexpected issue. This could save the entire project and possibly even your job. Being effective in problem solving is definitely something you need to keep close to you. It will not only help you in those situations, but assist you in making better and stronger decisions.

# Chapter Seven: Team Mental Models

In 1990, the term, team mental model was created to represent the fluid dynamics of effective teams. Researchers wanted to know exactly what made them such an effective team. This research also helped us to understand large and complex situations and how teams functioned within them.

A team mental model is defined loosely as a group's shared, organized understanding, and representation of key parts of the team's relevant environment. From this, the thesis that a teams effectiveness will improve if the team members inside are on the same page mentally and continuously. These people would also be held to a higher standard when it came to calming the group around them, explaining the processes, and keeping a peaceful group atmosphere. It is understood that a team that had a congruent understanding of the tasks were capable of interpreting other members actions better than if the team did not have a fluid understanding across the board and stood without a shared mental model.

Mental models within a team dynamic allows for a direction of processes and created an atmosphere of enablement for the team members within to create task predictions. It becomes a bit more complicated because each of the individuals within the team need to, not only focus on solving the task at hand, but doing so while coordinating a large group of people to stay on the same track. Mental models don't just play an important role in everyday functions, but they also create more healthy emergency responses. Because they are all following the same mental path flow, they can anticipate each other's movements and questions when there isn't enough time for explanations.

While teams all over the world are using a plethora of different mental models to complete their work and bring the group together, two main types of mental models are focused on for research purposes, task forced and team focused. The research on the usefulness of team mental models can get confusing. It's not only hard enough to study large groups interacting using mental tools, but many of the scientists behind the different studies use different matrix to measure the accuracy and development of the studies.

One popular way of studying the effectiveness of mental models within a team environment is to collect ratings from participants through quick, intuitive judgments in regard to similarities of concept pairs. These judgments are transformed into graphs on an individual basis and then are able to be compared through statistics and data comparison charts. Team mental models like concept mapping and performance adjustments have recently been used in order to measure the actual effectiveness of teams in real-world situations where they had to work together to finish a project.

Ultimately, researchers are hoping that the use of mental models within group environments, especially those where one or more of the team members is participating remotely, will help to create symbiotic and high performance results within companies. Due to the argument that team actions and behaviors cannot be studied until we understand the cognitive process in the team as a whole, the use of mental models has become an excellent way to continue to study the project processes of group projects.

Teams are not only pertinent to the working arena but to schools and education as well. Those in the educational field are often faced with the same issues that those in the working world are.

The types of team mental models are the same that individuals have used for decades only broadened to fit a large group of people. They quickly found that education on whatever type of model the team would be using was pertinent, but once they were hooked into each other, things rolled pretty smoothly. Team members were automatically on the same processes and able to put out their thoughts and ideas based on the fact they were all presented at once. This allowed for far more options then one person could come up with in the same amount of time. Group settings also allowed for a broad range of expertise to be present, helping to fade away some of the personal bias that was occurring.

It is too early in the lifespan of team mental models to tell if it will be more or less productive than individual usage, but more and more companies are adopting the practice, and modifying the base mental models to fit the team dynamics within the company project processes. Only time what the real hard research data will reveal, but if you are participating in a team mental model environment, there are three main best practices that can be put into place to make the most out of your team sessions.

# Mental Model Team Best Practices

A team operating under a collection of individual mental models, all conforming to the same rules and structure, can either look like a free flowing, fully functioning, organism or a pile of humans, smacking into each other, fumbling the data, and wasting enormous amounts of time trying to simply sort through the logistics before even touching the project and information. For those in a free flowing form, by adding discipline to the decision-making, there are three best practices that can give your team an edge in the high-performance realm.

## Roles

When you are dealing with a group of people, it is so important to make sure that every last one of them knows exactly what their role is within the group. When someone is lost, or there are positions not filled that are needed, then frustration and irritation can bring the group dynamic to a screeching halt.

A popular method of assigning roles is RAPID, or recommend, agree, perform, input, and decide. This process isn't always perfect but it definitely keep the groups from missing pieces of the puzzle that will later throw everyone off track. In RAPID the recommenders are those that make the proposal alternatives. They need access to data and they personally need to have common sense about what's practical and effective in the situation.

Those that are labeled to agree, are the ones that have to sign off on all decisions before the group can move forward. If the people with the agree power, veto something from the recommender, then it moves over to the decision makers. Those with the veto power are limited and are usually legal or compliance within the company.

The input people are consultants. They provide the information and facts that everyone will need to make an informed decision. Usually those that would be implementing the change are the ones providing the input. They all try to come to an agreement on the basic point and decision. However, the "D," or decision maker, is the one who has to ultimately commit the company to the decision.

Finally, there are those that perform. These people are actually, physically performing the decision. They make sure that the decision is fully implemented correctly and in a timely manner. This is the most crucial role within RAPID. They believe that a good decision put into the works quickly is better than a brilliant one put into motion slowly and without thought.

## Input then Share

Just as they hoped they would, companies that use decision-making teams have an extreme power to widen the perspective of the entire project. They have been known to even triple the number of ideas and choices that were being put up for discussion. This is very vital to the process. The more ideas they have, the more likely they will be to find the perfect resolution for the issue. This is why the individuals give their input before the team comes together as a whole. The two questions asked are:

- What goals are the most vital for the decision?

- What choices, out of the selected are the most realistic?

This enables the leaders to get everyone's information and ideas into writing. Just by having that, the amount of people breaking into arguments significantly decreased. The written words were for the people with a multitude of communication styles. Once the information was together, then it was shared with the entire team. The team is asked their own set of two questions.

- What parts of the information pop out?

- What sections, facts, or ideas are missing?

These steps become the basis for the group mentality and the way they will function through the entire rest of the process.

## What, Why, and How

Buy-in is critical to making any large organizational change effort happen. Unless you win support for your ideas, from people at all levels of your organization, big ideas never seem to take hold or have the impact you want. Our research has shown that 70% of all organizational change efforts fail, and one reason for this is executives simply don't get enough buy-in from enough people, for their initiatives and ideas. Kotter, para. 3, (2011)

Real buy-in from those higher up in the company would be impossible without sharing the details of the decisions and why the group made them. Oddly enough this step is often forgotten about either due to the excitement of coming to a decision, or because the quality of it was poor. Team decisions have to be high quality, founded in nothing but facts. If the team is asked why and their answers are based on "feelings," or they begin to struggle to answer the question, the buy-ins will not happen.

The communication of team decisions not only shows the competency of the team, but allows the team to go back and thank each and every member of the team for their contributions. These feelings of comradery inside of the team make the team buy-ins higher, even when the decision isn't a fully shared agreement. In the end, everyone comes together as one collective unit, standing behind one agreed upon ideal.

As you can see, the team aspect of mental models seems to be moving forward just as the individual mental model popularity had before. While it is much more difficult to establish real explainable data for teams, this hasn't stopped corporations from moving forward with training and know how. The group mentality has been an ever expanding realm of the corporate world. While it doesn't focus on the small companies out there, the model would be perfect to help those small companies grow larger.

But what about the individual? Has the growth in the mental models stopped? Are individuals stuck cycling through the mental models in existence, and eventually pushed into a group setting? With the ability to challenge your own mind, you are ultimately challenging your mental models. These mental models can shift as they are just thoughts in your head. But what happens when those thoughts turn into a completely new way of thinking?

# Chapter Eight: Challenging Mental Models And Your Own Thought Process

As children many of us are taught to not speak unless spoken to. We are told to hold our tongues, to respect our elders, and to respect authority. We move through our youth and into our adult years, now pros at holding back our thoughts and feelings on certain things because we don't feel as if we have a place to say anything. Our first jobs come and go and we sit through the rough times, knowing we have fully thought the issues at hand through, but we didn't have the background or the experience to make our thoughts be known.

This is a mental model in itself. The somewhat self-imposed, somewhat societal imposed view of where we stood in the world compared to corporate America. Their pressed white shirts, colorful ties, and strong frowns struck fear into us. The fact that our bosses were fearful of them too only cemented the idea further into our psyches.

James R. Detert and Amy C. Edmondson conducted a study on the systematic fear of employees to speak up to their bosses. They began the study by interviewing 200 individuals from all levels of a leading high-technology corporation. The company itself had put a lot of work into ensuring there were avenues for employees to speak up about any serious problems occurring in the company. They provided ombudspersons as well as a very thorough and in depth grievance procedure.

However, out of the two hundred people surveyed, half of them still said that they did not feel safe to speak up about the company or challenge their way of doing things. The surprising part was that they weren't concerned with complaints, but instead, reluctant to share their creative ideas on how to improve products, processes, and performance. Detert and Edmondson, in the article, Why Employees Are Afraid to Speak, published in the Harvard Business Review, gave a sad but truthful explanation for this.

Detert and Edmondson believed that it was ultimately self preservation that kept employees from speaking out. It is not just complaints or whistle blowing it is also information that would eventually lead up to positive changes for the organization. To people, sharing their ideas, with the possibility of backlash was very personal. But the ideas they had, actually implemented into the company, seemed too outlandish to really worry about. Therefore, people just played it safe. They kept their ideas to themselves.

Employees had no real proof that the higher ups would find fault in their sharing of ideas, but the fear was still there. Some believed that the higher up would resent them, since they had taken ownership of the project. Others believed that their bosses would feel betrayed or embarrassed to have a lower employee offer important suggestions to those higher than themselves. None of these beliefs, however, had a single shred of proof or fact behind them. It brought a very clear and discouraging realization to Detert and Edmondson.

Their findings told them that encouraging employees to speak out isn't just about taking away the barriers for them to do that. And it's also not about putting systems in place. That comfort to make an employee feel safe about expressing their opinions, concerns, and recommendations take a huge cultural shift within the organization. Ultimately that shift will change the way that people understand the personal costs versus the benefits of doing so.

While the management and higher ups at this and other companies obviously have quite a bit of work to do, encouraging the staff to open up with their ideas, the employees of this company and many more need to start understanding that this mental model isn't working for them. They need to break that chain and evolve their state of mind.

# Individual Ability to Change Our Personal

# Mental Model

All throughout this book we have talked about learning new Mental Models in order to implement them at work, at home, anywhere. But just because Mental Models offer the opportunity for advancement and thorough decision making skills, does not mean that they are all positive. Remember that mental models in theory are simply our assumptions from societal learned behavior, our values, our beliefs, and our experiences, rolled together in order to dictate us how we understand the world around us.

But, if that mental model is dictating a distorted view based on all the things above, then it is our responsibility to change it. To challenge the idea that we constructed our original mental model with. However, we do know that this can be a tall order. Our brains are powerful organs, seemingly holding onto the things that have been in our minds the longest.

In 2011 Peter Senge and his colleagues illustrated how our own social biases can be then sewn and built into our brains. Senge used the "Ladder of Interference," originally proposed by Chris Arhyris. The image below shows the loop that our minds go through on a regular basis. As human beings, we should be basing our thoughts and ideals on careful consideration, facts, and situation, we are instead fearing that change.

# The Ladder of Inference

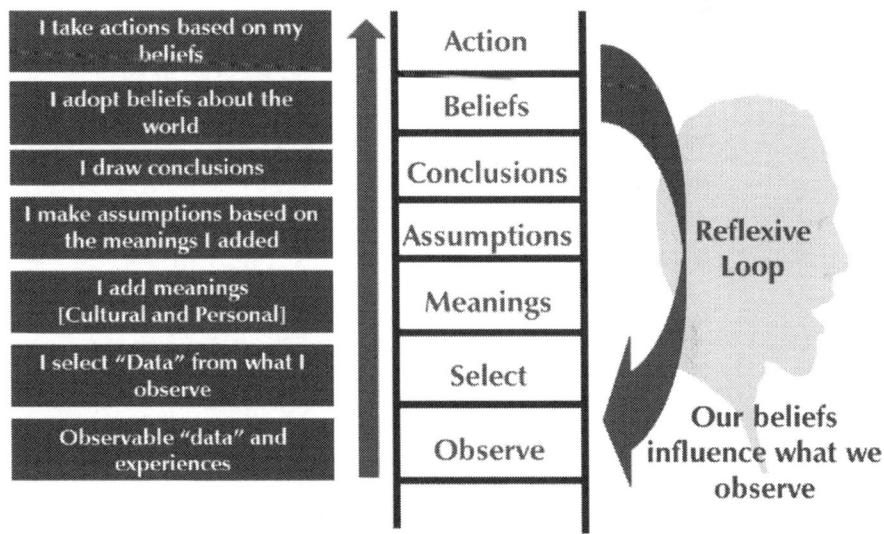

It is possible though, to break this endless cycle. Just like smokers tell their brains no more, like dieters turn away from the sweet treats, we too can adjust our brains to think how we want them to think. However, it will take more than courage to begin seeing these self-deprecating ideals just slip away. We need to begin restructuring our mind to fit, not what society tells us, not what fear tells us, but what want to see our of ourselves. Create a new mental model just as you want to see it, without thought or question. Senge stated that:

- Every important decision we make usually goes through this cycle:

- Taking actions based on my beliefs,

- Adopting beliefs about the world,

- Building conclusions,

- Drawing assumptions based on meaning,

- Adding meanings,

- Selecting information that you observe, and

- Observing information and experiences. Senge et al (2011)

This latter can also work as a reflective loop. See, beliefs are influenced by what we observe around us. We then very often draw conclusions based on our own beliefs and assumptions are usually seem so blatantly obvious. But without thinking we actually just jumped right into them. Those that start at the top of the ladder have no fear, diving off the end and into their fearlessness and privilege. But Senge asked the question, "What if we started at the bottom?"

According to him, we could change the way that we are focusing our attention. From a cultural stance, when a person adopts a meaning from, we have this automatic tune dial that pushes us right into ourselves. But we want to hear what others say. Even in this scenario the person might still keep their feelings and thoughts to themselves. You have to break the cycle. There is no gentleness to it. According to Senge you can begin to challenge your beliefs through the following:

- Being aware of our thinking (asking ourselves provoking questions and reasoning)

- Showcasing our advocacy (using examples, facts, and information gathering)

- Inquiring into others' thinking (having a meaningful dialogue when challenging our own and others' points of view)

- Interpreting the meaning (for ourselves and resisting jumping to conclusions based on what we think others meant)

When we are able to become aware of our mental models, we ask ourselves what led us to this way of thinking or feeling, and whether the results intended were achieved? Challenging your beliefs and assumptions is never easy, but can be achieved using:

Ask Questions

Work Together

Pay Attention to your Personal Effect on Others

Once you have been able to mold yourself into the person you want to be, using the mental model as both a shackle holding you back and a catalyst for the future, you can begin to change the things you want to see differently in the world around you. You can create a safety for yourself and a motivation for others. Lead by how you want to be treated. Clearing those roadblocks and hurdles could open you up to far more advanced discoveries and theories as you will be able to work through the bias.

# Conclusion

It seems we have come to the end of *Mental Models: The Secret Weapon to Master Problem Solving, Boost Your Productivity, and Make Better Decisions.* We hope that you were able to capture solid information that can assist you in improving your own processes as well as your teammates. It's almost enlightening to find out that the biases in our minds are not abnormal at all in human beings. That we all have a story, but that story does not have to define us in the future. The tactics and best practices you have just read through will allow you to drown out that subconscious thought and focus solely on the decisions and problems that you are facing. It will allow you to remember the important goals in your life so that you can be as productive as possible.

Our brains, full of vitality and always yearning for more information, no longer have to be classified as stubborn or controlling. When you are able to take control of your own mind, and implement the tools to create pathways to better time management, cleaner desks, and thorough input and output within your mental models, you become free to push forward in your personal life and your professional one. You don't have to be weighted down by the ideals that were pushed into you as a child, you can be your own person. Even the biased thoughts simmer in your head, you will be in control over your life, your body, and everything you had planned for the future.

The mental model's structured internal framework allows us to move through and process decisions and issues anytime and anywhere. Once you are mastering those tasks, you can begin to spread out, creating your own mental models to specifically fit the problems and your brainstorming tactics perfectly. Almost every product in the country is fitted for personal taste, why wouldn't the one thing we create on our own be the same? Remember to always keep that glossary of mental models locked up in your brain so you are quickly and efficiently able to implement the one that works the best with whatever situation you are facing. Let's take a quick review of what we went through in Mental Model: The Secret Weapon to Master Problem Solving, Boost Your Productivity, and Make Better Decisions.

We started the discussion from the very basics of Mental Models, and that was defining exactly what they were and what they were used for. Those problem solving techniques are tried and true, having helped to create solutions to problems spanning the ages. Even our own system of financial wealth was deeply affected by mental models, giving rise to financial empires and personal wealth beyond most people's comprehension. Even if the weren't officially named, mental models have been part of the human psyche since our creation.

Within Chapter One we learned about the psychological aspects of mental models and how they affect our psyches. We learned about the seven Principles of Reason, the basis to the continuing research into mental models by the psychological research community. This chapter gave us a full understanding of the inner workings of mental models and how the implementation of them in our private and professional lives can give us an edge on productivity, problem solving, and decision making. They why's of mental modeling are now completely laid out so that you understand the pertinent nature of their construct within our society. With the broad spectrum of industry and science that implement and study mental modeling, you are almost certain to come in contact with their functions and placement at some point in your career and life.

Having a solid understanding and full comprehension of the

background of these models you can now begin to connect the dots to the thousands of different classifications of the tools. You will be able to implement them into your daily routine, your large scale projects, and your everyday decision making processes and all without anything other than you own brain. Most people won't even know that you are implementing these time tested processes, but they will begin to see your ability to bring forward the best options, decisions, and productive reasoning that is available. Not only did it not cost you a dime, but it could push you higher up in your professional career, as well as your personal financial independence.

The versatility of the mental model structure can range from difficult and complex to extremely simplistic, allowing anyone, at any age, from any walk of life to use them in their daily chores. The information in this book took any doubt from your mind that you could implement the processes yourself, and show you exactly how to do so in the most efficient manner. In Chapter Two we explained how, through mental modeling your vision could be changed and perfected using specific but simple techniques. You began to understand that the process you used when making all the decisions you have made up to that point were all based around a very simple example of metal modeling created by you during the course of your life. And now you know, you're not confined to just that mental model anymore.

Chapter Two dove into the concept of immersing yourself in the different variations of mental moods. Those variations are now allowing you to take your own evolved mental model and create opportunities to open up the broad arena of options when making decisions, strengthening your productive mindset, and facing problems head on. You are beginning to open your mind to a world of information and opportunity that hadn't been accessible before. You can now find color to your flat unassuming process of decision making, bringing options and color to the projects you work through.

It is true, sticking with one method of modeling can bring down an idea, goal, or even company. Having blinders on leaves you with little choices for growth, both personally and professionally. The mental models that you are beginning to test out in your own mind are showing you the pathway to the broader thought process. Further into Chapter Two we talked about several of the more widely used mental models and the principles of each one. Common knowledge and its often negative thought process on the creative mind was discussed as we attempted to show you how your own mind may have been blocking opportunities in the past. We thoroughly discussed diversification, game theory, anchoring heuristic, the illusion of control, tribalism, working backward, and homeostasis. From there it is up to you to continue to explore the thousands of other modeling options out there, or even begin to create your own.

We, as human beings, evolved, traveling by rockets to the moon, curing diseases, discovering species so small only technological advances could see them, still have something we share with our Neanderthal brothers and sisters. We have the same exact brain. Our human brains have not evolved from the first human being, but the way we use them, and our ability to reason has. Cognitive bias, however, has become stronger since the beginning of human life. With the complexity of the society we have created for us, we are more likely to have stronger cognitive biases than any other human generation in history, and it will only get worse. That is why fully understanding Cognitive Bias is pertinent but also why there is no use looking behind you into the past, wondering what decisions you might have made differently had you known. What has been will stay and your only option is to move forward with this new tool and ability.

Chapter three helped you understand the infinite universe of knowledge and how our cognitive bias actually takes up space that could be filled with opportunities and options instead of fears, judgments, and personal opinions. You will now begin to understand the overload of information and the tools you can use to simmer that, pull the pertinent information from it, and extrapolate only the data you will need to fill your mental model and find those options that you need to complete your projects successfully. Those chemical endorphins you once got thinking about your next vacation or the gossip column in your local paper will now be pumping around the ideas and processes that you are able to create using mental modeling.

The four main causes of cognitive bias need to be considered by you on a daily basis. You need to take the concepts learned in this chapter and remember them. That way, when you are in a brainstorming session, using mental modeling, you are able to push aside the distractions that usually plague you and continue forward.

The multitude of ways that our own cognition, our past, our learned behaviors can distract us from our daily lives. You can now see how they become a distraction and how that not only affects the amount of information you are sifting through as well as your ability to focus. Since mental modeling can be processed anywhere at any time, allowing you to push back those biases even before you begin structuring your model for processing.

Confirmation bias can be a heavy player in your modeling processes. Releasing the need to hold onto the information you thought was truth, can put you at a disadvantage. If you add a weight into the process, you may be unable to look past the main components of the project. This brings you right back to the start. But now you have a really good understanding of the most widely infecting cognitive biases. We discussed Ambiguity Effect, Confirmation Bias, Availability Heuristic, Halo Effect, the Self-Serving Bias, Attentional Bias, Actor-Observer Bias, Functional Fixedness, Anchoring Bias, Misinformation Effect, False Consensus Effect, Optimism Bias, Automation Bias, and finally, Courtesy Bias.

Taking a step back out of your own head allows you to see the biases for what they truly are, manifestations of years of societal constructs etched into your mind. Change them. Make them into the types of functional processes that you need to rid yourself of these thoughts and memories. Use your strength, experience, and wisdom to change the way your mind actually processes. With this you will now be able to push past any biases that your mind has refused to let go of and improve your quality of life, relieve that unneeded stressors, and improving on the work environment that you spend years with.

Cognitive bias is a very in-depth category of the human psyche. It doesn't just affect your mental modeling, but with the ability to recognize your own biases, you may be able to fix the other aspects of your life that were touched by these biases. The processing speed of these mental models are going to be completely up to you and how you want to process them. But regardless of the small details, you know that even when you are on the go, you will be able to do that freely, without the stress of bias on your back. You can use your basic human skill of productivity, problem solving, and decision making to create opportunities for yourself and for your family. The sheer depth of the mental model can be intimidating but the beautiful thing about it is your new ability to appreciate it, but still control yourself and step through one moment at a time.

The problem you have on your hands will be the first thing that you will always define. From that, using knowledge, and inference, you will be able to begin the process of pulling these issues, problems, and decisions apart. However, you know that you don't have to be so proficient and in depth when it comes to the smaller processes in life. There is no need to create a specialized mental model and begin breaking down the process of grocery shopping or laundry. Those things, and all of the little stuff, can continue to be taken care of by the initial mental model that you have had your entire life. While it most likely will change over time as your biases disappear and your realization of the process grows stronger, it is meant for the simple tasks.

The generation of solutions, after understanding the scope of the project or issue you are facing, could take a while depending on how much information you have gathered. That information became those solutions. If you were to go with the first possible solution that popped into your head, you could cheat the process of a possible perfect answer to your decision or project. Once the plethora of solutions are gathered, then you simply choose the best solution and implement it. This whole process could take days or it could literally take just a few seconds. This is why the simplest form of your mental model should be used for inconsequential questions or decisions.

The Productivity and two of the Mental Models that were used the most were the Pareto Principle and the 2-Minute Rule. They can give a good solid base for you to come from, moving right into the problem solving realm of things. The Inversion Mental Model and Occam's Razor are skilled and unforgiving in their implementation but can bring you some of the best problem solving techniques out there. Make sure to study their implementation before trying them out on any problem of dire circumstance. That goes the same for decision making process.

The background and history of Warren Buffett gave you a break from the technical to really see how implementation of solid business practices combined with theoretical theories played a huge role in his success. He was and is just a man, a man that used the mental models amongst other psychological theories to change our financial system and history for years to come.

Throughout the book you learned implementation techniques, best practices, and most importantly things to avoid in order to stay successful in your strides toward problem solving and decision making success. We got a glimpse at the world of team mental models, and discussed the challenge that mental models placed on your own thought process. Remember, nothing in your biases are irreversible. You have to study and trust the process, keeping your eye out for those distractions and biases that sneak up on us when we least expect it.

We hope that you enjoyed this book, finding a solid grasp on the process of mental models, best practices, avoidable actions, and everything in between. Whether you are a CEO or a Mom at home, mental models can be pertinent in your own life.

---

*If you enjoyed this book and you want to learn more about Self Confidence, Self Discipline, and Self Esteem, check my others book browsing "Charlie Holl" on Amazon. Thank you!*

# References

Baron J (1994). Thinking and deciding (2nd ed.). Cambridge University Press. ISBN 978-0-521-43732-5.

Barron, B. (2000). Achieving coordination in collaborative problem-solving groups. Journal of the Learning Sciences, 9(4), 403–436.

Benscn, Buster. "4 Basic Problems Cause All the Cognitive Biases That Screw up Our Judgment." Business Insider, Business Insider, 25 Mar. 2017, www.businessinsider.com/4-basic-problems-cause-all-the-cognitive-biases-that-screw-up-our-judgment-2017-3.

Berkshire Hathaway Inc. to Acquire Burlington Northern Santa Fe Corporation (BNSF) for $100 Per Share in Cash and Stock". Business Wire. Retrieved June 24, 2019.

Bossche, Piet Van den, et al. "Team Learning: Building Shared Mental Models." SpringerLink, Springer Netherlands, 17 Mar. 2010, link.springer.com/article/10.1007/s11251-010-9128-3#cities.

Boyd, Stowe. "Decision Making, Not Decision Faking." Clover Pop, Erik Larson-Clover Pop, 2017, www.cloverpop.com/hubfs/Whitepapers/%20Cloverpop_Decision_Making_White_Paper.pdf.

Box, George E.P.; Meyer, R. Daniel (1986). "An Analysis for Unreplicated Fractional Factorials". Technometrics. 28 (1): 11–18. doi:10.1080/00401706.1986.10488093.

Buffett, Warren. "Chairman's Letter-1996." Chairman's Letter - 1996, 1996, www.berkshirehathaway.com/letters/1996.html.

Buffett, Warren E. (October 16, 2008). "Buy American. I am. " The New York Times. Retrieved December 25, 2012.

Buffett, Warren. "Three Lectures by Warren Buffett to Notre Dame Faculty, MBA Students and Undergraduate Students." Edited by Whitney Tilson, Tilson Funds, 1991, www.tilsonfunds.com/BuffettNotreDame.pdf.

Buhayar, Noah (September 20, 2013). "Buffett Calls Federal Reserve History's Greatest Hedge Fund". Bloomberg. Retrieved September 20, 2013.

Bunkley, Nick (March 3, 2008). "Joseph Juran, 103, Pioneer in Quality Control, Dies". The New York Times. Archived from the original on September 6, 2017. Retrieved 25 January 2018.

Campbell, Arianna. "5 Mistakes to Avoid When Problem Solving." Boomer Consulting, Inc., Boomer Consulting, Inc., 11 July 2017, www.boomer.com/single-post/2017/07/11/5-Mistakes-to-Avoid-When-Problem-Solving.

Cherry, Kendra. "How Cognitive Biases Influence How You Think and Act." Verywell Mind, Verywell Mind, 7 May 2019, www.verywellmind.com/what-is-a-cognitive-bias-2794963.

Clear, James. "How to Stop Procrastinating by Using the '2-Minute Rule.'" James Clear, 13 Nov. 2018, jamesclear.com/how-to-stop-procrastinating.

Clear, James. "How to Train Your Brain to Think in New Ways." James Clear, 1 Sept. 2018, jamesclear.com/feynman-mental-models.

Clifford, Catherine (February 26, 2018). "Berkshire Hathaway's Warren Buffett remembers meeting Charlie Munger". Cnbc.com. Retrieved March 11, 2019.

Delane, Juntae. "10 Things To Avoid If You Want To Be Productive." Digital Branding Institute, 18 June 2015, digitalbrandinginstitute.com/10-things-avoid-want-productive/.

Detert, James R., and Amy C. Edmondson. "Why Employees Are Afraid to Speak." Harvard Business Review, Harvard, 1 Aug. 2014, hbr.org/2007/05/why-employees-are-afraid-to-speak.

Dictionary, Business. "Productivity." BusinessDictionary.com, 2018, www.businessdictionary.com/definition/productivity.html.

Driver, Cab. "Warren Buffett's 2-List Strategy to Prioritize and Focus." Medium, Publishous, 17 Nov. 2018, medium.com/publishous/warren-buffetts-2-list-strategy-to-prioritize-and-focus-3832a6c70311.

https://www.forbes.com/sites/eriklarson/2017/05/18/research-reveals-7-steps-to-better-faster-decision-making-for-your-business-team/#2e786a9940ad

Education, Eller Executive. "Problem Solving Best Practices." Eller Executive Education, Eller, 28 June 2019, executive.eller.arizona.edu/2017/11/21/problem-solving-best-practices/.

Farrington, Robert. "The top 10 investors of all time". The College Investor. The College Investor, LLC. Retrieved November 20, 2015.

Frost, Aja. "Mental Models: The Ultimate Guide." HubSpot Blog, 13 Sept. 2018, 12:03am, blog.hubspot.com/marketing/mental-models.

Gerasimova, Kate. "How to Challenge Your Mental Models and Think Differently." GothamCulture, 23 Mar. 2017, gothamculture.com/2017/03/23/challenge-mental-models-think-differently/.

Johnson-Laird, P., Girotto, V., & Legrenzi, P. (2005, 3 18). http://www.si.umich.edu/ICOS/gentleintro.html   Retrieved

from                                    http://www.si.umich.edu:
http://www.si.umich.edu/ICOS/gentleintro.html. Second link
as           first         no           longer          works:
http://musicweb.ucsd.edu/~sdubnov/Mu206/MentalModels.
pdf

Johnson-Laird, P. (2013). Mental models and cognitive
change. Cognitive Psychology, 131-138.

Kelly, Rod. "The Mental Model of Attribution Theory (Aka
'Cause Theory') in Business." Rob Kelly's Blog, 17 Mar. 2017,
robdkelly.com/blog/mental-models/attribution-theory-in-
busines/.

L, Scott. "An Overview of the Mental Model Theory."
LessWrong        2.0,        17        Aug.        2015,
www.lesswrong.com/posts/YKCoj7DxDMktr4qKP/an-
overview-of-the-mental-model-theory.

Larson, Erik. "3 Best Practices For High Performance
Decision-Making Teams." Forbes, Forbes Magazine, 9 Oct.
2018,    www.forbes.com/sites/eriklarson/2017/03/23/3-best-
practices-for-high-performance-decision-making-
teams/#f30b98ef971b.

Larson, Erik. "A Checklist for Making Faster, Better
Decisions." Harvard Business Review, Harvard, 17 Jan. 2019,
hbr.org/2016/03/a-checklist-for-making-faster-better-
decisions.

Larson, Erik. "Don't Fail At Decision Making Like 98% Of Managers Do." Forbes, Forbes Magazine, 18 May 2017, www.forbes.com/sites/eriklarson/2017/05/18/research-reveals-7-steps-to-better-faster-decision-making-for-your-business-team/#2e786a9940ad.

Marshall, Perry (2013-10-09). "The 80/20 Rule of Sales: How to Find Your Best Customers". Entrepreneur. Retrieved 2018-01-05.

Morlok, Becky, et al. "INTERVIEW: Dr. John Kotter on Creating Organizational Change." Hr Bartender, 29 Oct. 2018, www.hrbartender.com/2011/business-and-customers/interview-dr-john-kotter-on-creating-organizational-change/.

Nersessian, N. (2002). The cognitive basis of model-based reasoning in science. In P. Carruthers, S. Stich, & M. Siegal, The Cognitive Basis of Science (pp. 133-153). Cambridge University Press.

Pareto, Vilfredo; Page, Alfred N. (1971), Translation of Manuale di economia politica ("Manual of political economy"), A.M. Kelley, ISBN 978-0-678-00881-2

"Psychology." Psychology, 2019, psychology.iresearchnet.com/industrial-organizational-psychology/group-dynamics/team-mental-model/.

Q, A S. "What Is Problem Solving?" ASQ, ASQ, 2019, asq.org/quality-resources/problem-solving.

Rana, Zat. "The 10/10/10 Method: Make Decisions Like Warren Buffett and Ray Dalio." Medium, Personal Growth, 23 Feb. 2018, medium.com/personal-growth/the-10-10-10-method-make-decisions-like-warren-buffett-and-ray-dalio-99e4857d05e3.

Robert G. Hagstrom. "The Warren Buffett Way". Wiley Publishers. P. 29. Retrieved May 6, 2016.

Rogers, Paul, and Marcia W. Blenko. "Who Has the D?: How Clear Decision Roles Enhance Organizational Performance." Harvard Business Review, Springer Link, 8 Jan. 2019, hbr.org/2006/01/who-has-the-d-how-clear-decision-roles-enhance-organizational-performance.

Streets, Farnam. "Inversion: The Power of Avoiding Stupidity." Farnam Street, 31 Aug. 2018, fs.blog/2013/10/inversion/.

Street, Farnam. "The Danger of Oversimplification: Use Occam's Razor Without Getting Cut." Farnam Street, 31 Aug. 2018, fs.blog/2017/05/mental-model-occams-razor/.

"The World's Billionaires". Forbes. March 5, 2008. Retrieved May 20, 2008.

UMass. "Decision-Making Process." Decision-Making Process

- UMass Dartmouth, University of Massachusetts Dartmouth, 2017, www.umassd.edu/fycm/decision-making/process/.

Unknown. "A Very Useful Work of Fiction – Mental Models in Design." The Interaction Design Foundation, 2011, www.interaction-design.org/literature/article/a-very-useful-work-of-fiction-mental-models-in-design.

User, Super. "What Is Productivity." Ministry of Employment, Immigration, and Civil Status, Republic of Seychelles, 2012, www.employment.gov.sc/what-is-productivity.

Vozza, Stephanie. "15 Habits That Will Totally Transform Your Productivity." Fast Company, Fast Company, 23 Aug. 2018, www.fastcompany.com/3051540/15-habits-that-will-totally-transform-your-productivi.

Writing Lab, Purdue. "Fallacies // Purdue Writing Lab." Purdue Writing Lab, Purdue University, 2015, owl.purdue.edu/owl/general_writing/academic_writing/logic_in_argumentative_writing/fallacies.html.

Yates, Jim. "Ladder of Inference." Pivotal Thinking, Fulcrum, 2011, pivotalthinking.wordpress.com/tag/ladder-of-inference/.

Zhang, Yu, et al. "A Preliminary Research on Modeling Cognitive Agents for Social ..." Mafiadoc.com, MAFIADOC.COM, 2006, mafiadoc.com/a-preliminary-

research-on-modeling-cognitive-agents-for-social-
_59c14fd21723dde3106b047d.html.

Made in the USA
San Bernardino, CA
07 September 2019